EDGES OF HIS WAYS

EDGES OF HIS WAYS

Selections for Daily Reading

FROM THE
NOTES OF
AMY CARMICHAEL

A DOHNAVUR BOOK

CHRISTIAN LITERATURE CRUSADE
Fort Washington, Pennsylvania 19034

CHRISTIAN LITERATURE CRUSADE
Fort Washington, Pennsylvania 19034

First published in 1955
Seventh impression 1970

First American Edition 1975

Reprinted by permission of S.P.C.K.
Holy Trinity Church
Marylebone Road, London N.W. 4RU

SBN 87508-064-2

EDITOR'S FOREWORD

THESE notes of Amma's[1] covered a number of years—those years in which she was unable to have much contact with her beloved Dohnavur Family. They also covered a number of needs of which she was always lovingly aware.

In order to try and fill the lack caused by her apartness from their daily life, she wrote or dictated frequently, and often daily for long periods, some word for them that she had asked the Lord to give. Even though apart from them, she lived very close to their needs, and she knew that the way of help for them lay in her closeness to Him. "As for me, nearness to God is my good" was very true of her.

She always reminded us that what He gives is never for ourselves alone, but is given to be shared; and this little book holds a selection of what she shared with us through the years, without, of course, any thought of publication.

They have not been taken in their chronological order, but chosen and edited with the hope and prayer that they may find a need, and therefore a response, in the hearts of our "larger family", some of whom have asked for them.

The title is from Delitzsch's translation of Job 26. 14: "These are the edges of His ways", and indeed she recognized in all He gave, only the edges of the Greater Power behind and beyond, and with Job realized that they were merely "whispers", as compared with it.

In thinking these thoughts with her, may our hearts be as ready as hers was, to take what He offers so abundantly for our help—help not for ourselves alone, but to be shared, that freely as we have received, so we may freely give.

---

[1] Amma—the name by which Amy Carmichael was (and is) widely known.

NOTE

AMMA read very widely, and often quoted from what she had been reading. It has not been possible to identify all the quotations in these messages, though we have tried to do so.

With regard to the different versions which are made use of, Amma wrote herself, in 1932:

> In case any are puzzled by the different translations from which I draw strength and help and delight, it is like this: In studying any object with the microscope we use different lenses and turn the mirror in various ways; each change brings out some new wonder and beauty. So it is for those who are not Greek or Hebrew scholars, and who use the work of scholars to open the meaning of the inexhaustible Word—the Bible is richer than any single version can fully show.

The different versions and sources referred to in abbreviated form are:

A.V.	=	Authorized Version.
R.V.	=	Revised Version.
P.B.V.	=	Prayer Book Version, the Great Bible (Miles Coverdale, 1488-1569).
LXX	=	Septuagint.
Am.R.V.	=	American Committee's 1901 Edition of the R.V.
Kay	=	Dr W. Kay's Version of the Psalms.
Weym.	=	Weymouth.
Way	=	Dr Arthur Way's Letters of St Paul.
Roth.	=	Rotherham.

Verses of Poetry not in inverted commas, are from Amma's own writings, unless otherwise stated.

Dan. 1. 5 :   *And the king appointed them a daily provision of the king's meat.*

And if that king did so, how much more ours.

Give us this day our daily bread.

Psalm 104. 28 : *Thou openest Thine hand, they are filled with good.*

What a God! Let us live rich lives to-day.

JANUARY 1

Rock of my heart and my Fortress Tower,
  Dear are Thy thoughts to me,
Like the unfolding of leaf or flower
  Opening silently.
And on the edge of these Thy ways,
  Standing in awe as heretofore,
Thee do I worship, Thee do I praise,
  And adore.

Rock of my heart, and my Fortress Tower,
  Dear is Thy love to me,
Search I the world for a word of power,
  Find it at Calvary—
O deeps of love that rise and flow
  Round about me and all things mine,
Love of all loves, in Thee I know
  Love Divine.

JANUARY 2

Deut. 11. 11, 12 : *From the beginning of the year even unto
the end of the year.*

I do not know why these words came with such strong consolation this morning, but they did. I had been thinking about
Renewal, and wondering how it was there was such continual
need of it; we drink and are satisfied; our thirst is quenched,
and we live again, gratefully conscious of an inward renewal of
hope and joy and courage. And then, next day, perhaps even
only an hour later, we need to drink again if we are to go on
at all. It was then that these words came like the sound of
bells.

"From the beginning of the year even unto the end of the
year"—much is folded up in that. The day of the week, the

1

hour of the day, every minute of the day, not one is outside
His care—"a land which the Lord thy God careth for; the
eyes of the Lord thy God are always upon it, from the beginning of the year even unto the end of the year"—and so "it
drinketh water from the rain of Heaven". It need never
thirst.

JANUARY 3

Psa. 90. 17 : *Let the beauty of the Lord our God be upon us.*
Psa. 27. 4 :   *One thing have I desired of the Lord, that will I*
    seek after; that I may dwell in the house of the Lord
    all the days of my life, to behold the beauty of the
    Lord.
Zech. 9. 17 : *How great is His goodness, and how great is His*
    beauty.

And this God is our God. Let us be glad in Him to-day,
and stay where we can see His beauty.

> One thing have I desired, my God, of Thee,
> That will I seek—Thine house be home to me.

> I would not breathe an alien, other air,
> I would be with Thee, O Thou fairest Fair.

> For I would see the beauty of my Lord,
> And hear Him speak, Who is my heart's Adored.

JANUARY 4

A few days ago, I looked out of my window in the early
dawn and saw the branches of the tamarind trees against a sky
of gold. And it struck me afresh that every night, however long
and difficult, ends in a dawn of gold.

This reminded me of Julian of Norwich and of how she
wrote, "It is God's will that we take His comfortings as largely
and as mightily as we may take them, and also He willeth that
we take our troubles as lightly as we may take them, and set
them at nought."

Psa. 30. 5   Yes, for "joy cometh in the morning".

JANUARY 5

Isa. 64. 5: *Thou meetest him that rejoiceth and worketh righteousness, those that remember Thee in Thy ways . . . in those is continuance.*

Three conditions, two assurances. If only we will be happy, work, and remember our loving Father, He will meet us in His ways, and those ways will not end in a blank wall, a precipice, darkness; in those (ways) is continuance.

This word has strengthened me afresh. Many things end— hopes, plans, powers—but not the eternal leadings of the Lord our God. The path leads on through plain and valley and forest, up to the heights. The way is like the sunlit patch on the sea at dawn. It "shineth more and more unto the perfect day." And then?   Prov. 4. 18

JANUARY 6

Psa. 31. 19: (Rotherham) *How great is Thy goodness which Thou hast hidden away for them who revere Thee.*

We do not see it all now, it is hidden away, kept for a surprise of love.

"He hath made wonderful His loving kindness for me in a   vv. 20-21
fortified city." What is my city to-day? What are my circumstances? Just where I am He waits to make His loving kindness wonderful to me.

> Whoso hath known that comforting,
>   The inward touch that maketh whole,
> How can he ever choose but sing
>   To Thee, O Lover of his soul?

JANUARY 7

Psa. 45 :   *A Song concerning the Beloved.* (The title as given in the Septuagint.)

Psa. 40. 17 : *The Lord thinketh upon me. The Lord will take care of me.*

Two dear and lovely things from my Quiet this morning: "A Song concerning the Beloved"; "The Lord will take care of me."

We have many songs concerning our Beloved; we often sing them, and listen to them being sung. All such songs were written in the Heavenly places where we "sit" when we are nearest to our Lord. In no other place can a true song concerning the Beloved be written. In no other place can it be truly sung of Him or truly sung to Him. It is a Heavenly thing from beginning to end. That is why to sing it, or to hear it sung, is the joy and the rejoicing of our heart.

But sometimes such a joy is penetrated by a question like a spear-point : It is so to-day, but what of to-morrow? What if I, who have sung a song concerning the Beloved, fail Him in the end?" This is the answer, the sure and blessed answer to the tempter who always, if he can, interrupts the sweetness of our songs : "The Lord thinketh upon me"—"the Lord will take care of me", even of me. Is that not enough?

JANUARY 8

2 Sam. 7. 25 : *Do as Thou hast said.*

This morning, just as if read for the first time, the words "Do as Thou hast said" brought a deep sense of restfulness.

David was thinking about his kingdom. We may be thinking about the great dark world, or about ourselves and our strangely persistent need of grace, strength and guidance. Whatever be the subject of our thoughts, we are met by the eternal promises of God, promises that exactly meet our need. And how many so ever be the promises, we know that in our Lord Jesus Christ is the Yea, and through Him is the Amen.

2 Cor. 1. 20 R.V.

So all we have to do is to do as David did, take God at His word. We do not need to say much. With the confident simplicity of a very small child who has never heard of a grown-up breaking his word, we may say, "Do as Thou hast said."

JANUARY 9

The only thing that matters is to please Me.

Have you noticed that if you go to sleep with the thought of Him Whom your soul loveth, you waken—at least often it is so—with some little word from Him, a verse from His Book, or a hymn, or just a simple word that tells you nothing new, but somehow helps.

"The only thing that matters is to please Me," that was the word that woke me a few days ago, and it has not gone away. When the thought of the things that I cannot do comes and tries to trouble me, this little simple word comes at once. The other things *seem* to matter. I often think they do matter. But they are as though they did not matter in comparison with pleasing our Lord Jesus.

The word—that simple word—reminded me of those other words, "All that pleases is but for a moment. All that grieves is but for a moment. Only the eternal is important." Are any of you tried about anything? I think if you listen you will hear Him say, The only thing that matters is to please Me.

JANUARY 10

1 Sam. 23. 16 : *And Jonathan Saul's son arose, and went to David into the wood, and strengthened his hand in God.*

God make us all His Jonathans. There is a great hunter abroad in the world. Like Saul who sought David every day, he seeks souls every day, never a day's respite, always the hunt is on. Although the words stand for ever, "but God delivered *v. 14* him not into his hand", yet sometimes souls tire of being hunted, and like David they are in a wilderness in a wood. Then is Jonathan's chance. But notice what he does, he does not so comfort David that he becomes necessary to him. "He strengthened his hand in God." He leaves his friend strong in God, resting in God, safe in God. He detaches his dear David from himself and he attaches him to his "Very Present Help". *Psa. 46. 1* Then Jonathan went to his house, and David abode in the wood—*with God.*

JANUARY 11

Next time we read of David being in serious trouble he had no Jonathan to strengthen his hands. "And David was greatly distressed; for the people spake of stoning him. . . . *But David* *1 Sam. 30. 6* *encouraged himself in the Lord his God.*" Long afterwards when he was delivered from Saul he sang one of his songs, "It

Psa. 18. 32, 39, 46 is God that girdeth me with strength. . . . Thou hast girded me with strength. . . . The Lord liveth." (His dear Jonathan was dead, but he does not even speak of him, all that matters is, "The Lord liveth; and blessed be my Rock".)

If he had leaned on Jonathan, if Jonathan had made himself necessary to David, he would not have leaned on his Rock and proved the glorious strength of his Rock; his whole life would have been lived on a lower level, and who can tell how many of his songs would have been left unwritten, with great loss to the glory of God and to the Church of all the ages?

So let us not weaken those whom we love by weak sympathy, but let us love them enough to detach them from ourselves and strengthen their hands in God.

JANUARY 12

John 15. 12 : *This is My commandment, that ye love one another, as I have loved you.*

Was the love of Jonathan rather a cold kind of love, the love that does not care very much to be "loved back again"? 2 Sam. 1. 26 David did not think so : "Very pleasant hast thou been unto me : thy love to me was wonderful, passing the love of women." To love as Jonathan loved, and to show that love as he showed his, is not to be hard, or cold; it is not to give a stone when a hungry heart asks for bread.

We cannot love one another too much. It is impossible to love too much. "This is My commandment, that ye love one another as I have loved you." We cannot approach that, much less pass it, so we cannot love too much. Let all loving hearts then be at rest about loving. Only let the love be selfless, strong, brave, faithful. There are always chances for strengthening one another's hands in God; let us not lose our chances.

JANUARY 13

2 Sam. 9. 1,3 : *Is there yet any that is left of the house of Saul, that I may show him kindness for Jonathan's sake? . . . Is there not yet any of the house of Saul, that I may show the kindness of God unto him?*

Saul had not been kind to David, but all that is forgotten. David remembers the one lovely thing that came from that house. "Whatsoever things are . . . lovely . . . think on these things"; leave the rest—forget them—that is the word that shines forth here. *Phil. 4. 8*

Would it not be good to get into the way of looking out for chances to show kindness over and above duties? These words might be well written up, if not on the walls of our rooms, then on the walls of our hearts. "Is there any that I might show him kindness? Is there any that I might show the kindness of God unto him?"

Kind Father, teach us how to show Thy kindness.

JANUARY 14

Sometimes it is a help to remember that we are not the only people who have been tempted to be cast down. "And if I be cast down, they that trouble me will rejoice at it", is as true now as ever it was. But look at the words that follow. "My trust is in Thy mercy; and my heart is joyful in Thy salvation. I will sing of the Lord, because He has dealt so lovingly with me: yea, I will praise the Name of the Lord most Highest." *That* is where we are meant to live, and where we can live we will live. There is no provision in the whole Bible for a despondent Christian. "Thanks be unto God, Which always causeth us to triumph in Christ"—that is the word for us all. *Psa. 13. 4*

P.B.V. v. 5, 6

2 Cor. 2. 14

JANUARY 15

Rom. 16. 10: *Salute Apelles approved in Christ.*
Apelles, that tested man in Christ; "the Lord knows, not we, the tests he stood." (Moule)

Let us stop for a moment, and think what it would be if at the end of the day our name might be written thus: that tested man—that tested woman—that tested girl—that tested boy, in Christ. Would it not be joy past telling if only that might be? But to the tested man, woman, girl, boy, there is sure to come temptation to depression; and so in this same letter and in other letters, St Paul uses a beautiful, strong, heartening word, which in our Authorized Version is translated *comfort*, and which means not so much the consolation of grief, as "the encouragement which banishes weakness and depression." (Dr Griffith Thomas)

Let us be "comforted together" afresh to-day. We may all be His Apelles.

JANUARY 16

There are some things we never forget. They may pass out of the front part of our memory, but they are somewhere at the back and the least thing can recall them. The word "all", when I hear it read aloud, recalls this:

Some time after I heard, and for the first time understood and believed, that we could be kept from falling, I was at a big meeting in Scotland where Dr Andrew Bonar was speaking. He was very old and could not speak very plainly or strongly. The hall was full, and I was near the back. I could not catch a single word he said, except this word "all". He read 2 Cor. 9. 8 and he put every bit of strength he had into it, so that the one word rang out—*all*—*always*—*all*—*all*. I have forgotten thousands of great sermons but that "all" I have never forgotten, and it has helped me countless times. It helps me afresh to-day. "God is able to make *all* grace abound toward you; that ye, *always* having *all* sufficiency in *all* things, may abound to every good work."

All means all, not some; *always means always*, not sometimes. Lord, to-day help us to live upon this "all".

JANUARY 17

Deut. 32. 12: *There was no strange god with him.*

As that word was being read to me, the comfort of it came home to my heart. What would it be if one morning we woke up to find a strange god with us—a stranger, a foreigner, as the word means—one whom we did not know at all? What would it be? It will never be. "So the Lord alone did lead him, and *there was no strange god with him*." We may rest our hearts on that.

"In my flesh shall I see God, Whom I shall see for myself, Job 19. 26, 27 (and see mar.) and mine eyes shall behold and not another"—"not a stranger"—not a foreigner—not one whom I shall have to learn to know and love—but the God Who has led me all my life long, and not another. No strange face will meet us on that Day, we shall be awakened by the vision of His face—*His* face, not the face of a stranger.

A little girl was slowly dying in her worldly home in India, and a Christian doctor who was called to see her told her of our Lord Jesus. After a little while she began to understand and to love Him. One day she said, "I don't know anyone in Heaven. I shall feel very shy there." "But you know our Lord Jesus," said the doctor, "you won't be shy of Him," and she was comforted. Soon after that she saw Him—*not another, not a stranger*, but the Lord Who loved her and gave Himself for her.

JANUARY 18

Sometimes we think of the invitation of Matt. 11. 28 as if it had been spoken to sinners burdened by their sin. It is to them, of course, but not only (perhaps not chiefly) to them. That is why the words over the door of the House of Prayer are, Come to Me. Those dear words are to us all, and each time we cross the threshold of that House, our Lord says to each one—calling him and her by name—*Come to Me*.

In the Aramaic it is "Come unto Me, all you who are tired out and carrying burdens". Perhaps the burden that is tiring you out is not your sin (for that has been forgiven) but the sin of another, a soul dear to you. Sometimes it is the weariness of illness, or the tiredness after pain. Sometimes it is the inability to help others as you long to do; the burden of the loving heart can be a heavy burden. The words come fresh as dew to us every morning, "Come unto Me, all you who are tired out and carrying burdens, and I will give you rest."

JANUARY 19

I wonder if this will find anyone who is discouraged and afraid? From the beginning of the Bible to the end there are

Matt. 14. 27
John 14. 27

words of comfort and encouragement. We know that the temptation to fear is a very old one; millions of people have had it. But they have conquered, and so will you, if you take our Saviour's words of strength to yourself, and stay yourself on them. *Be of good cheer. Peace I leave with you, My peace I give unto you: not as the world giveth, give I unto you. Let not your heart be troubled, neither let it be afraid.*

JANUARY 20

Isa. 27. 8: *He stayeth His rough wind in the day of the east wind.*

"His rough wind". These words were a comfort to me this morning as I thought of all who are in pain, or any trial of the flesh. By the time that wind reaches any child of the Father it is *His* wind.

And "He stayeth His rough wind in the day of the east wind." Things will never be too hard to bear. "We are troubled on every side yet not distressed; we are perplexed but not in despair". I have been finding much food in 2 Cor. 4, strong food, and as I think of all who are out in the rough wind, *His* rough wind, I am comforted.

JANUARY 21

Some days are so thorny that one seems to be caught in a thorny bush and scratched all over. No sooner is one set of thorns dealt with than another set is in evidence. I do not think any of us find such days easy.

Deut. 33. 16
Roth.

But there is a word that speaks of the goodwill of One Who dwelt in the thorn-bush which may help through such days: "And with the precious things of the earth and its fulness, and with the goodwill of One Who dwelt in a thorn-bush." That One knows all about thorn-bushes. Thorns were His heritage. He chose them for His crown. And His goodwill is on His servant, and He will give light and strength to fulfil all His will. It was one who knew much of life's thorn-bushes who wrote,

We follow in His footsteps;
  What if our feet be torn?
Where He has marked the pathway
  All hail the briar and thorn.
Scarce seen, scarce heard, unreckoned,
  Despised, defamed, unknown,
Or heard but by our singing,
  On, children, ever on.

Ter Steegen

May the Lord in His infinite tenderness use this word to comfort someone who for His sake is in a thorn-bush now.

JANUARY 22

Matt. 8. 24, 26 : *There arose a great tempest in the sea . . .*
            Then He arose, and rebuked the winds and
            the sea.

The winds arose . . . He arose. I have been living on "When the waves arise, Thou stillest them", and so we are never overwhelmed.   Psa. 89. 9

There are almost always waves. Now and then we have times of quietness—little lulls, I used to call them—but far more often the wind is blowing from one quarter or another, and so there are waves, sometimes mighty waves of the sea. I have never known a time when it was not so, and do not think I ever shall. So let us make up our minds to it and have done with wishing that things were easier. They are not, and they will not be. (So long as we fight Satan he will fight us; if he does not, it will be because we are not worth fighting.) But that is not the whole story. The whole splendid story is just this, "O Lord God of hosts, Who is a strong Lord like unto Thee, or to Thy faithfulness round about Thee? Thou rulest the raging of the sea. When the waves thereof arise, Thou stillest them."

JANUARY 23

Psalm 73. 26 : *But God.*

These words have been like strong hands lifting up, bearing up, countless thousands of souls. "My flesh and my heart faileth : but God is the strength of my heart and my portion for ever." Many who will read this note are well and strong and joyful in their work, thank God for that. Sooner or later, however, to most who follow the Crucified, there comes a time when flesh and heart fail, and if it were not for that "But God", we should go under. Will those, to whom they are not the needed words to-day, take them and store them safely in the wonderful storehouse which God has given to us all—memory? And when they are needed they will rise up and speak.

That failing of flesh and heart belongs to the time when "there be many that say, Who will show us any good?" Feelings and fears can be like a torrent of rough water and we see no way to cross it. "But God" makes all the difference then, "for Thou, Lord, hast never failed them that seek Thee."

Psa. 4. 6

Psa. 9. 10
P.B.V.

JANUARY 24

Rev. 1. 16, 17 : *And He had in His right hand seven stars . . . And He laid His right hand upon me saying, Fear not.*

These words must have come to tens of thousands of the Lord's followers; the wonder of them and the dearness of them is fresh to-day as I read them. Do you not sometimes find yourself almost thinking, How can He, Who has the whole world to care for, attend to this tiny matter that troubles me? It seems almost unreasonable to ask for such attention. Sometimes it seems almost selfish. But here we have the truth we know so well in a great picture—the hand that holds the seven stars is the hand that is laid upon us—and the "great voice as of a trumpet" speaks softly to the inner ear of each one of us, saying unto us, saying unto you, saying unto me, "Fear not, I am the first and the last :" "the same yesterday, and to-day, and for ever."

Heb. 13. 8

JANUARY 25

Mark 6. 41 :   *He blessed and brake and gave.*
John 6. 12 R.V. : *Gather up the broken pieces that nothing
                  be lost.*

In England we cut a loaf, and if there is anything over, it is
a cut end of loaf, or there may be a few slices. There are never
"fragments" which the Revised Version renders literally
"broken pieces". But in India people break bits off a loaf or
cake, and I suppose it was so in Palestine, as broken pieces, not
slices, were left over of what the Lord had first blessed and
broken and given.

Some of us may be much more like poor broken pieces than
nice tidy cut slices. At any rate we feel so. Is it not a comfort
then, to read that not only did our Lord bless and break and
give, but every morsel of what He had blessed was, in His
sight, worth gathering up for use? We may be only the odds
and ends of things, not worth calling anything, but what He
has blessed He uses, that nothing, even such nothings as we are,
be lost.

JANUARY 26

For those who have to do with forgetful people.

"I have compassion", our Lord said as He looked at the
multitude. I have often found it easier to have compassion on
the multitude than on the individual, especially a rather tire-
some individual. But our Lord Jesus never failed in this keener
test of compassion.

You know how a tune heard before recalls, when you hear
it again, not only the place where you heard it, but all the
surrounding circumstances. It seems to me that when our Lord
used exactly the same words, "How many loaves have ye?" He
was trying lovingly to recall to the Twelve what they had
forgotten, even His boundless power and mercy.

When next we have to deal with a forgetful boy or girl,
perhaps this way of His will help to guide our ways. It is so
easy to feel inwardly impatient, but He Whom we follow never
did.

> "Jesus Master, I would be
> More and more made like to Thee."

Mark 8. 2

Mark 8. 5
Mark 6. 38

JANUARY 27

1 Kings 17. 7, 14, 16: *It came to pass after a while that the brook dried up. . . . Thus saith the Lord God of Israel, The barrel of meal shall not waste, neither shall the cruse of oil fail . . . And the barrel of meal wasted not, neither did the cruse of oil fail, according to the word of the Lord, which He spake by Elijah.*

Sooner or later all brooks of earth dry up. But the increase of meal in the barrel and of oil in the cruse was not of earth. Until the need ends, the supply of that which is divine will continue.

Heb. 4. 16 "Grace to help in time of need." Blessed be those words; I am not good at remembering references and I have often had to find them to make sure beyond a doubt that they were in the Bible, for they were so exactly what I wanted that I almost thought I must be making them up. But no, thank God, there they are, and never, never will any power on earth or in hell remove them from that place, or sap their strength, or undermine their truth.

JANUARY 28

1 Kings 18. 42 : *Ahab went to eat and to drink . . . Elijah went up to the top of Carmel.*

Every day we live we have to choose whether we shall follow in the way of Ahab or of Elijah. If we put self first, whether in great things or small, we are like Ahab. And the habit grows 1 Kings 22. 37 with life till we end as Ahab ended. "The king died and was brought to Samaria"—that poor little hill which never saw anything glorious till One, Who was wearied by His journey, sat on the well-side there.

If we put the things which concern the Kingdom first, then life will be a climb. Every day will see us higher up the mountain which is our Carmel; and in the end, even though a whirlwind does not carry us home, either angels, or our Lord Himself, will call us to meet Him in the air, far, far above

all mountain tops. We shall not be sorry then that we chose
Carmel.

JANUARY 29

1 Kings 19. 7 : *And the angel of the Lord came again the
second time, and said, Arise and eat; because the
journey is too great for thee.*

Is it not good and comforting to know that the angel of the
Lord came again the second time? We never come to the place
where we pass out of reach of the compassion of our God. "His   Lam. 3. 22, 23
compassions fail not. They are new every morning", never
tiring of us, always strong for our help.

There have been times for nearly all of us when we have
felt the truth of the angel's word, "The journey is too great for
thee"; but have we not always found the Bread of Life and the
Water of Life ready for our sustenance? And in the strength   1 Kings 19. 8
of that meat we have gone on, and shall go on, even unto the
Mount of God.

JANUARY 30

Lavish.

St Paul had a lovely way of letting his letters break into song
every now and then. (Way's translation shows this.) One line
in a song that comes in Romans 8 has been a great help to me.
Way calls the song a "Hymn of triumph to Jesus". This is the
line : "How can He [the Father] but, in giving Him, lavish on   *v.* 32
us all things—all?" "Freely give" means to give lavishly. What
do I need to-day? Strength? Peace? Patience? Heavenly joy?
Industry? Good temper? Power to help others? Inward con-
tentment? Courage? Whatever it be, my God will lavish it
upon me.

Sometimes it helps to look at something which is given to us
lavishly, and then to turn the thought upward and ask for, and
believe to receive as lavishly, that which we so much need.
Well, if in truth God is ready to give, not just a little, but
lavishly, whatever we need for victorious life, then it follows
that we need not fail. When we fail it must be that we have
put some barriers between ourselves and our supply.

I think it is here that we need to direct prayer, prayer against barriers, and these are nearly always made of self-love in one form or another. God save us from that, and enable us to receive that which He so lavishly gives.

JANUARY 31

Joshua 3. 4 : *Ye have not passed this way heretofore.*

Did you ever notice this verse in any special way? As each new day begins it is true to say, I have not passed this way heretofore; joys that I never met before will meet me to-day; surprises are awaiting to delight me. But other new things will meet us : new temptations, or old ones with new faces, new difficulties, too, perhaps new trials. We have not met any of them before, but look at verse 11: "The Ark of the Covenant of the Lord of all the earth" passed over before the people into Jordan. That was enough to make everything right then. It is Exod. 33. 15, 14 enough to make everything right now. "If Thy Presence go not with us, carry us not up hence." "My Presence shall go with thee, and I will give thee rest." Strength and peace are in that kind of rest.

Ye have not passed this way heretofore. This is a new day for you, but He Who loves you meets you at the gate of the Psa. 29. 1 day, and at the gate of the new month, and He says, Fear not, the Lord will give you strength : the Lord will bless you with peace.

FEBRUARY 1

Psa. 1. 6 : *The Lord knoweth the way of the righteous.*

Those who read (as part of their reading) in any appointed course, such as the Psalms for the day, know what it is to look forward to welcoming some familiar beloved word which they know will be waiting for them, as sure and as shining as the coming of the stars in their order.

Psalm 1 seems to be the perfect psalm for the beginning of a new month, because of *v.* 6, "The Lord knoweth the way", the way through this new month, the way through this new day.

I find from Young's Concordance that the word used for "way" here means "trodden path", but this new month, this new day, is an untrodden path for us. We have not passed this way heretofore. How then "trodden"?

The Bible is full of surprises. They belong to "the delightfulness of the Lord" that we see if we dwell in His house all the days of our life. This delight is a new one to me, and it is delight to share it. The word "trodden path" is the word used in the prayer, "Teach me Thy way, O Lord, and lead me in a plain path", a *trodden path*—a Leader always goes before, and so the path is trodden.

Psa. 27. 4
Roth.

Psa. 27. 11

FEBRUARY 2

Psa. 85. 13 : *Righteousness shall go before Him; and shall set us in the way of His steps.* (The "trodden way".)

Blessed be God for such words, and blessed be the love that divides up the journey of life into steps, such little things, like minutes, to which indeed they correspond.

To-day, with its many minutes, lies before us: joyful, painful, peaceful, assaulted, anxious (for others not for ourselves), relieved, praiseful minutes. The painful minutes will be helped

17

if only we refuse to be occupied with pain, and look instead at the Feet that tread the path step by step (minute by minute), for they are wounded Feet. The joyful minutes will be hallowed by the remembrance that for every golden minute the price of Blood was paid; joy unhallowed by that thought is as the crackling of thorns under the pot. And all the other diverse minutes will be triumphant, steps that are set in the footprints that lead on in the path-way of His blessed Feet.

FEBRUARY 3

Luke 4. 30 : *Jesus passing through the midst of them went His way.*

Our new month will bring us joys, for the Lord of joy is with us; it will also bring us sorrows, for sorrows are part of life.
v. 29 It may bring things which would "throw us down" if they could. But they need not ever do that, for it is possible for us to do just what our Master did when, passing through the midst of them, He went His way.

As, by His grace, we go on in quietness, we shall find those
Exod. 33. 14 words we know so well come true : "My Presence shall go with thee, and I will give thee rest."

FEBRUARY 4

A man who often had to meet difficulty has said that "difficulty is a severe instructor. He that wrestles with us strengthens our nerves, and sharpens our skill. Our antagonist is our helper."

Let us not be surprised when we have to face difficulties. When the wind blows hard on a tree, the roots stretch and grow the stronger. Let it be so with us. Let us not be weaklings, yielding to every wind that blows, but strong in spirit to resist.

> Strong in the Lord of Hosts,
> And in His mighty power;
> Who in the strength of Jesus trusts
> Is more than conqueror.
>
>   *C. Wesley.*

FEBRUARY 5

1 Chron. 12. 14 : mar : *One that was least could resist an hundred, and the greatest a thousand.*

This verse has helped me very much, and others also to whom I have given it; it was the word *resist* in the margin that the Spirit used to strengthen me.

Some of us feel indeed "one of the least", and yet by the grace of God we can resist, and resist not one or two of the inward foes that are sure to try to weaken us every day we live, but a hundred of them. There are no limits set to the power of God given to the least of us. It was these least of David's army who joined with the greatest—those who could resist a thousand—and went over Jordan when it had overflowed all its banks. So let us go on resisting—*even unto the end.*

FEBRUARY 6

Sometimes we are tempted to make much of trifles, and even to speak of our "sacrifices". David Livingstone suffered every sort of trial that men could suffer in opening Africa, and some of those trials he had to mention, but he added : "I do not mention these privations as if I considered them to be *sacrifices,* for I think that the word ought never to be applied to anything we can do for Him, Who came down from Heaven and died for us."

FEBRUARY 7

Do something for others.

Habakkuk must have been feeling rather downhearted when he began to write his book. There was a great deal to make him feel so. But he set himself to listen to what his Lord had to say to him, and the first words he heard were not about himself at all, but about others. He was told to go and write something in large letters, perhaps on stone, so that people who ran past could read it.

When you are feeling downhearted, go and do something for others. If you do that, and go on doing it, you will come to the place where Habakkuk was when he wrote his glorious

Hab. 3. 17, 18 *Yet.* "Although the fig tree shall not blossom, neither shall fruit be in the vines; the labour of the olive shall fail, and the fields shall yield no meat; the flock shall be cut off from the fold, and there shall be no herd in the stalls : *Yet* I will rejoice in the Lord, I will joy in the God of my salvation."

Think of the grit of that man long ago. He did not wail about feelings. And his God is your God. He can make even you a Habakkuk.

FEBRUARY 8

Luke 22. 43 : *And there appeared an angel unto Him from Heaven, strengthening Him.*

John 16. 33 Just a little while before that He had said, "I have overcome the world"; and yet there was need for special strength, and His Father sent an angel to strengthen Him.

This has been a word of peace to me to-day. We accept our Father's will, and know that He has given us the victory over all the power of the enemy. Nevertheless there are times when we do need special strength if we are not to break down before the end. Our Father knows this; He does not say, You accepted all at the beginning; this that tries your spirit now was included in that.

His love understands and He sends an angel to strengthen us.

FEBRUARY 9

Deut. 1. 28 : *People greater and taller than we;*
            Cities great and walled up to heaven;
            Moreover we have seen giants. (Young)

Rom. 4. 19
R.V. Faith does not hide difficulties or belittle them. "Without being weakened in faith Abraham considered . . . "; let us not fear to consider what we are up against :

     i. as Christians—"principalities and powers mustering their unseen array";

     ii. as winners of souls—cities, as it often seems, walled up to heaven, so impervious do they seem, like the temples of India with their high double walls. As missionaries, incidentally, we know what it is to feel the language like a city with very high walls.

iii. Moreover on every side we have seen giants—giants of ancient deep-rooted wrong.

But let us look up. What are all these things—peoples, cities, giants—to the Lord our God?

The Lord your God Who goeth before you, He shall fight for you.   *v. 30*

FEBRUARY 10

Luke 12. 32 : *It is your Father's good pleasure to give you the Kingdom.*

These words have been life to me many a time, and have held me steadfast. Not the devices of the enemy, but our Father's good pleasure must be accomplished. That word was rock.

So when we are facing the impossible, we can count upon the God of the Impossible.

How can we fear?
For love delighteth ever
To meet our need,
And great it is indeed,
For we go forth
To meet a foe who never
Before mere man doth
    cower.
But God, our Tower,
Is our Defence, He is our
    Power.

Our fingers He
Doth teach the art of fight-
    ing.
His bugle call
Hath summoned soldiers all
To rise and go,
In faith and love uniting.
This war is His affair,
Unseen as air,
Upon the field He will be
    there.

FEBRUARY 11

Psa. 18. 1, 2 : *I will love Thee, O Lord, my Strength. The Lord is my Rock, and my Fortress, and my Deliverer; My God, my Strength, in Whom I will trust; my Buckler, and the Horn of my Salvation, and my High Tower.*

2 Sam. 22. 1

This is David's glorious song spoken "in the day that the Lord delivered him out of the hand of all his enemies". The form we have in 2 Sam. 22 Revised Version adds two words after "Deliverer"—they are *even mine*. "The Lord is my Rock and my Fortress and my Deliverer, *even mine*". Even mine, though I am what I am. Even mine, though I have to confess

Psa. 18. 17

so often that my strong enemies were too strong for me. O blessed be the love that draws the weakest of us into its embrace. "The Lord is my Rock and my Fortress and my Deliverer— *even mine*".

FEBRUARY 12

Psa. 63. 9
P.B.V.

I wonder if any of you are wanting just a word of pure comfort. If you are, you will find something very good in one of the Psalms for the day : *My soul hangeth upon Thee: Thy right hand hath upholden me*. This is the oldest version that is in common use now, and I think that it is one of the most beautiful of all. Will you let the comfort that God has for you in it lift you up and make you strong?

> In shadow of Thy wings I'll joy;
> For Thou mine help hast been.
> My soul Thee follows hard; and me
> Thy right hand doth sustain.
> > Metrical Version.

FEBRUARY 13

Psa. 68. 28 : P.B.V. *Thy God hath sent forth strength for thee.*

Many of us know what it is to receive a word in the early morning that lasts all through the day. We live on that word;

Psa. 37. 3
R.V. mar.

we "feed on faithfulness".

These few words from the Psalm for the day have been with me all through the hours. "Thy God hath sent forth strength for thee". The day lies before us. It will bring us things that in ourselves we have no strength to meet. That does not matter. Our God has already sent forth strength for us. It is like that

Psa. 59. 10
Amer. Ver.

other word, "My God with His lovingkindness shall come to meet me." Strength and lovingkindness—what more do we need? That duty, that difficulty, which we see coming to meet us, what of it? Our God hath already sent forth strength for us, and before the thing we fear can meet us on the road, our God with His lovingkindness shall meet us there.

FEBRUARY 14

Psa. 119. 105 : *Thy word is a lamp unto my feet, and a light unto my path.*

To-day, the word of light to me was a word very familiar to you all, but take it for yours as I took it for mine, and you will find it as welcome as the lamp which somebody brought that night to the jailor in the prison at Philippi : "He giveth power to the faint; and to them that have no might He increaseth strength . . . They that wait upon the Lord shall renew their strength; they shall mount up with wings as eagles; they shall run, and not be weary; and they shall walk, and not faint."   Acts. 16. 29   Isa. 40. 29, 31

> Bear us on eagles' wings,
>   Lord, lest we faint,
> Far, far from grovelling things,
>   Purge from their taint.
> Jesus of Calvary,
> Draw us to run after Thee,
> Hold us to walk with Thee,
>   Walk, and not faint.

FEBRUARY 15

Psa. 34. 4, 6 : *From all my fears . . . Out of all his troubles.*

My fear is not yours, but nearly everyone has, somewhere inside, a weary little fear which keeps cropping up. But every time the fear pushes out its head, there, waiting to end it, is that glorious word, "delivered from all my fears." (Not from some, or from most, but from *all*.)

Out of all his troubles : this may find someone in trouble. We may have to pass through the waters, but we shall be delivered out of them. They will not overflow us. "This poor man cried, and the Lord heard him, and saved him out of all his troubles." There again, it is not out of some, or out of most, *but out of all.*

FEBRUARY 16

Isa. 30. 18 : *And therefore will the Lord wait, that He may be gracious unto you, . . . blessed are all they that wait for Him.*

Did you ever put these two "waits" together like that? Perhaps there is a fear at the back of your mind just as a fear is sometimes at the back of mine. Perhaps nobody knows of it, or would only smile if they heard it. Never mind : read these words and let them lead you into peace.

FEBRUARY 17

Luke 3. 17 : *He will throughly purge His floor.*

Luke 3. 17

I have a word of comfort for all who feel as if they will never be what their Lord wants them to be, and what they themselves want to be. It is, "He will throughly purge His floor". If only we spread out our whole being before the Lord, He will throughly deal with everything in us which is chaff in His eyes. The means which He uses are compared to the searching forces of wind and fire. We must not try to keep anything from the wind and the fire. If we are open like a threshing-floor, then nothing can hinder our Lord in His throughly purging work. One more word of comfort; the fan that makes the wind is in His hand—the hand that was wounded for our transgressions—and fire is only another name for burning love. "From His right hand went a fiery law for them. Yea, He loved the people".

Deut. 33. 2, 3

Whatever the means of our perfecting may be, they come by way of His hand.

FEBRUARY 18

Song of Songs 5. 1 : *I have gathered my myrrh with my spice; I have eaten my honey-comb with my honey; I have drunk my wine with my milk; . . . drink, yea, drink abundantly, O beloved.*

There is much happiness in our lives. Sometimes it is as if our Lord filled us so full of happiness that there was very little of the cup and the baptism. But yesterday it came to me with a startling sense of utter truth, that in the cup filled with spices, honey, wine and milk, there was also myrrh; and myrrh, as we know, always speaks of suffering and death.

The call of our Lord is to "joy unspeakable and full of glory", the very wine of life. There is sweetness and nourishment—honey, and milk. There is all that "spices" mean, too. But there is also myrrh. No one who follows the Crucified is called only to life's delights, nor would he wish to be. When we taste the myrrh, do not let us forget the loving words, "Drink, yea, drink abundantly, O beloved." Let us not drink unwillingly, but with a generous trust in the love that says, *I* have drunk of that cup; drink, O beloved.

1 Pet. 1. 8

FEBRUARY 19

John 12. 3 : *The house was filled with the odour of the ointment.* Rotherham has, *"the fragrance of the perfume."*

Fragrance is like light. It cannot be hidden. It is like love, intangible, invisible, but always at once recognized. And its opposite is just as impossible to hide, and though it is neither to be touched, nor heard, nor seen, we know that it is there.

This brings us to a solemn truth : it is what we *are* that tells. I do not know any truth more searching. It sends us to the cleansing Blood, to Calvary. But it sends us to that house in Bethany, too, where Lazarus was, whom Jesus raised from the dead, the house which was filled with the fragrance of the perfume. I have been thinking of all the scattered houses here and overseas where any of us are. Lord Jesus, Thou hast come, not as Guest, but as King, to our house to-day; all that we are we pour on Thy feet. Let the touch of Thy blessed feet turn our poor offering to something sweet to Thee and to others— for Thy Name's sake.

FEBRUARY 20

Song of Songs 1. 3 : *Thy Name is as ointment poured forth.*

Have you ever tried to get something out of a bottle without taking the cork out first? Some people remind me of bottles with the cork in. There is something truly good inside but it is corked up. It cannot get out for the help of others.

Do you feel sometimes like a corked-up bottle? It is a stuffy uncomfortable sort of feeling, but some manage to get on like that for months on end, to their great loss, and the loss of all who have to do with them.

Dear corked-up bottles, do go and get uncorked! There is only One Who can take out the cork of self-love, or shyness, or sleepiness, or whatever it is that keeps you from pouring out for others all you have been given. He Who was always sweetness poured forth ("Thy Name is as ointment poured forth"), He can uncork your bottle, and then all you are and have will be used in the joyful service of others.

FEBRUARY 21

Matt. 28. 20 : R.V. mar. *Lo, I am with you all the days, even unto the end of the world.*

This promise of the Risen Christ turns our thoughts to the manifold vicissitudes of life in which the Lord is still present with His people.

"He does not say simply *always*, as of a uniform duration, but *all the days*, as if He would take account of the changing aspect of storm and sunshine, of light and darkness, which chequer our course." (Westcott.)

Bishop Moule interprets it, "all the days, and all the day long."[1]

FEBRUARY 22

Num. 7. 9 : *Upon their shoulders*

The Princes of the Tribes brought six covered wagons and twelve oxen for the service of the Tabernacle. Those wagons

---

[1] "I do not think that I refine too much when I say that the original of *all the days*, by the extending power of the accusatives, may justify this paraphrase."

were given to the Levites, that is to the sons of Gershon and
Merari, to every man according to his service; but to the sons   Ch. 7. 9
of Kohath no wagons were given, "because the service of the
Sanctuary belonging unto them was that they should bear
upon their shoulders."

Those men were human. I wonder if they were ever tempted
to wish they could have wagons. They also were grandsons of
Aaron. Why must they carry those heavy burdens on their
shoulders when their cousins had bullock-carts? If such
thoughts ever came, perhaps they found help in remembering
that to them was committed the care of the most precious   Ch. 3. 31
things, things too precious to be carried in any other way.

Is it not so even now? The burdens we have to carry on our
shoulders are what our God counts the most precious.

The Shepherd took the lost sheep—and a sheep is a heavy
thing—and laid it on His shoulders. If the Good Shepherd asks
us to bear upon our shoulders the care of souls, surely it is
because that burden is too precious to be carried in any other
way.

FEBRUARY 23

For those on whom burdens are laid

Num. 11. 14 : *I am not able to bear all this people alone,
because it is too heavy for me.*
1 Kings 19. 4 : *It is enough.*

Have you ever said so? I have. But we never know how
tender our Lord can be till we feel like that. He never meets
such words with coldness, He never misunderstands. His angels
are like Him in this. As God had seventy good men ready to
help Moses, so the understanding word of a kind angel to the
tired Elijah was "the journey is too great for thee." The angel
knew where to find a cruse of water, and flour to make a cake,   1 Kings 19. 7
and he had a little meal ready for him when he woke. And—
perhaps this mattered most of all—he knew he had need of
a good sleep.

When you feel at the end of everything, do not hesitate to
say so to your Father. If you listen you will hear Him say,
"Now shalt thou see what I will do"; and if you watch you   Exod. 6. 1

will see, as if newly created, all sorts of surprises of His love, comrades alongside, food and drink—the Bread of life and the Water of life.

FEBRUARY 24

Phil. 4. 5 : *The Lord is at hand.*

Rather a lovely thing happened yesterday evening. Someone had come to say Goodbye. He had been telling me of the loneliness of his life as a Christian in the Army. I had been telling him of the word upon which I had fed all day, "The Lord is at hand" (near, close to one's hand), when, without thinking, I stretched out my hand, and immediately he stretched out his, caught mine and held it. It came to me then so simply, and yet with much power and sweetness, that this little incident was indeed a figure of the true. If, instead of him, the Lord Jesus had been sitting in that chair, and I had stretched out my hand, would He not have done just what that dear boy did? And is this not what truly *is*, not in sight as yet, but in fact?

Am I weak, almost beginning to sink; burdened perhaps by my own troubles, perhaps by the troubles of others; blown about by stormy winds? When Peter saw the wind boisterous, Matt. 14. 30, 32 and was beginning to sink, he must have stretched out his hand as one does on such occasions. "*Immediately* Jesus stretched forth His hand and caught him, and said unto him, O thou of little faith, wherefore didst thou doubt?"

"And the wind ceased."

FEBRUARY 25

Quietness — Dew — Quietness.

Num. 11. 9 : *And when the dew fell upon the camp in the night, the manna fell upon it.*

Exod. 16. 13, 14   "In the morning the dew lay round about the host. And when the dew that lay was gone up, behold, upon the face of the wilderness there lay a small round thing, as small as the hoar frost on the ground."

In Dr Hertz's beautiful Pentateuch, he tells of the Jewish thought about the manna. First the dew fell; then the manna over the dew; then the dew again over the manna. If this be so, what a lovely figure of the true it is; first quietness—then the heavenly food—then quietness again. This touches our every morning Quiet Times, and especially our Lord's day, even though for many it is full of service.

Bishop Handley Moule used to say, Even if you have not a long time to spend in the morning with your God, *hem it with quietness.*

FEBRUARY 26

Psa. 1. 3 : *His leaf also shall not wither.*

"Quicken me" is repeated nine times in Psa. 119, and "quicken", Young says, means "keep", "preserve", as well as "make live".

I am often very glad the Bible is not afraid of appearing to contradict itself. There are days when we can sing and feel that our leaf "shall not wither"; these are "watered garden" days. There are other days when we feel like any old bit of dried-up grass. Blessed be God for the truthful Psalms.

So this word "quicken Thou me" carries two streams of living water. Are we rejoicing in a sense of life? Then, Lord, *keep* that which Thou hast given. Are the hot winds blowing? Then, Lord, make me to live "as Thou usest to do unto those that love Thy Name"—"according to the custom". It is our dear Lord's custom to look upon us, to turn Himself unto us—to quicken us. What a comfort such words are in arid days. "Thy word hath quickened me" : and all is well again, for He has come.

Psa. 119. 132
R.V. mar.
see R.V.

> "How entered, by what secret stair
> I know not, knowing only He was there."
> *T. E. Brown*

FEBRUARY 27

Deut. 8. 3 : *He suffered thee to hunger, . . . that He might make thee know that man doth not live by bread only . . .*

I wonder if any of us are tried by dryness? There must be a blessing in it or it would not be allowed, and certainly it is allowed at times. "He suffered thee to hunger".

I think one reason is that given in the words, "And fed thee with manna that He might make thee know that man doth not live by bread only, but by every word that proceedeth out of the mouth of the Lord doth man live." There is manna in Psa. 143 for such times. The truth-speaking soul opens its case to its God; no covering, no excusing, no pretending that there is not dryness: "Therefore is my spirit overwhelmed within me; my heart within me is desolate." Then follows the way out, "I remember the days of old; I meditate on all thy works; I muse on the work of Thy hands." What has God done? Remember *that*. Take time to meditate, to muse. Do not hurry. Let the Holy Spirit have time to remind us of the work of His wonderful hands.

Then "I stretch forth my hands unto Thee: my soul thirsteth after Thee, as a thirsty land." "Thou, O Lord, art the thing that I long for." Naught else can satisfy. But Thou canst, Thou dost; "Am I not enough, Mine own? enough, Mine own, for thee?" Yes, Lord, ten thousand times enough. Thou hast been yesterday, Thou art to-day, and Thou shalt be for ever, eternally, El Shaddai—the God Who is enough.

v. 4

v. 5

v. 6
Psa. 71. 4
P.B.V.

FEBRUARY 28

Deut. 1. 30: *The Lord your God Who goeth before you, He shall fight for you.*

Thank God for the battle verses in the Bible. We go into the unknown every day of our lives, and especially every Monday morning, for the week is sure to be a battle-field, outwardly and evidently, or inwardly in that unseen life of the spirit, which is often by far the sternest battle-field for souls. Either way, both ways, "The Lord your God Who goeth before you, He shall fight for you".

Then comes a word which I think will bring some of you (as it has me) a very tender comfort, for the Spirit of God goes on to speak of the wilderness and what happened there: "Thou hast seen how that the Lord thy God bare thee, as a man doth bear his son" ("as a nursling").

v. 31

LXX

Has He not done so through all the wilderness days that we have ever known? Will He not do so through any dry places that may lie before us? Then is there anything, can there be anything, to fear? We are His soldiers, thank God for that; we are His nurslings, too. We are never too grown-up to be, as Brother Lawrence puts it, "extremely caressed by Him."

FEBRUARY 29

Psa. 51. 12: (Rotherham.) *And with a willing spirit wilt Thou uphold me.*

These words helped me very much to-day. There may be many things ahead that look difficult (and are difficult). We want to be willing for them and perhaps do not see quite how we can be, or we fear to fail in inward willingness. *But the Lord will not fail.* "With a willing spirit wilt Thou uphold me."

MARCH 1

Fear not.

I am more and more impressed as I read the Bible, by the reiterated "Fear not". There are so many promises, that it would not be strange if there were no "Fear not"; the promises are enough to rest upon. We should not need to be told not to be afraid, and yet there it is over and over again, in one form or another, this strong, loving, encouraging "Fear not" of our God. "Fear not, nor be afraid;" *neither be cowardly* (it is good sometimes to face the truth that yielding to fear is cowardice); "it is the Lord your God that advances with you in the midst of you, neither will He by any means forsake thee, nor desert thee . . . And the Lord that goes with thee shall not forsake thee nor abandon thee."

Deut. 31. 6-8
See LXX

It seems to be God's plan to allow all sorts of things to happen that would naturally cause fear, but to forestall them by the assurance of His presence. *The Lord thy God, He it is that doth go with thee; He will not fail thee, nor forsake thee,* so, *Fear not, neither be dismayed.*

MARCH 2

Psa. 60. 12 : P.B.V. *Through God we shall do valiantly: for it is He that shall tread down our enemies.*

We are always learning something new when we read our Bibles, and I had not noticed till this morning, when I read again Psalm 60, that the Psalm which tells us to show our colours (display our banner) is the Psalm which tells us we shall do valiantly, for it is God that shall tread down our enemies.

Is there any one who needs to fear after reading such words as these? Each of us has something to do which is not easy. God takes care it shall be so. If things were easy, where would

32

be the fight? How should we be trained for Heavenly service?
But there is no need *ever* to be overcome. God makes provision
for victory, never for defeat.

MARCH 3

But if we are defeated? *There is forgiveness with Thee, that
Thou mayest be feared.* When I was small I used to wonder   Psa. 130. 4
why the word *feared* was used there, why not *loved*? But the
Spirit of God chooses the words He uses in the Scriptures, and
there is a solemn truth in this word "feared". Some of us know
what it is to have a child speak lovingly after being forgiven,
and yet perhaps that child does that same wrong thing again,
without apparently very much caring that it will need forgiveness again, and without in the least thinking of what its sin
has cost, and what forgiveness costs. So here the word strikes a
deeper note. "Feared" means "reverenced", it means "the
deep awe, which love so tender, yet so holy, must needs   Kay, note.
inspire." It means the kind of love which has fear and reverence
in it, and that kind of love will never think it is a little thing to
grieve our holy God.

If we have been defeated, let us not be discouraged, there is
forgiveness. But do not let us think lightly of defeat, as though
it did not much matter. It cost God Calvary to forgive my
"smallest" sin.

MARCH 4

Psa. 145. 14 : P.B.V. *The Lord lifteth up all those that are
        down.*

There is a wonderful uplift in being well and able for things;
in the bright beauty of the world in sunshine after rain; in the
love of those around us; in work that is the blessed gift of God;
in freshness of spirit and strength of body to do that work. In
spite of all these uplifting blessings I know well that there can
be temptations to downheartedness, and this little love-word
from this Psalm may be just the word for one of you.

Perhaps in the time when you are alone with your Lord
there may come that uplifting which is life and peace. It will

come by looking away from self to the Lord of Light and Joy. "They looked unto Him and were radiant."

Psa. 34. 5 Amer. R.V.

MARCH 5

Job 22. 29 : *When men are cast down, then thou shalt say, There is a lifting up.*

Eliphaz the Temanite said many unkind and untrue things. But he sometimes spoke truly, and this is a beautiful word of his : "When men are cast down, then thou shalt say, There is a lifting up". The people of God never should be cast down, never need be, and yet our Father knows that sometimes we are badly tempted in this way, "for He knoweth our frame; He remembereth that we are dust." I have noticed that in every age He has appointed some to say, There is a lifting up. Their lives say it. They are not bound and hindered by the things of time, they are not brought under the power of any of these things. They live in the world, buffeted by the winds of the world, and yet not cast down by them. Their very presence, the light in their eyes, the tone of their voice says, *There is a lifting up.* God make us all like that.

Psa. 103. 14

MARCH 6

Psa. 28. 9 : *Save . . . bless . . . feed . . . lift up . . .*

What an inclusive prayer! nothing is left out. The word that speaks to me specially is "feed".

I do not think there is anything from the beginning of our Christian life to the end, that is so keenly attacked as our quiet with God, for it is in quietness that we are fed. Sometimes it is not possible to get long uninterrupted quiet, but even if it be only ten minutes, "hem it with quietness." Enclose it in quietness; do not spend the time in thinking how little time you have. Be quiet. If you are interrupted, as soon as the interruption ceases, sink back into quietness again without fuss or worry of spirit. Those who know this secret and practise it, are lifted up. They go out from that time with their Lord, be it long or short, so refreshed, so peaceful, that wherever they go they unconsciously say to others, who are perhaps cast down and weary, *There is a lifting up.*

Job 22. 29

MARCH 7

James 4. 10 : (Rotherham) *Be made low in the presence of the Lord and He will lift you up.*

"Thou oughtest not . . . so to cleave to any heaviness, whereof ever it come, and take it as though hope of escaping were utterly taken away."[1] The way of escape is by way of the dust, down low at His feet we find *there is a lifting up.* — Job 22. 29

The Gospels give us a lovely picture of how we are lifted up. When Simon's wife's mother lay sick of a fever our Lord Jesus "came and took her by the hand, and lifted her up". It is always like that. — Mark 1. 31

MARCH 8

Psa. 147. 6 : *The Lord lifteth up the meek.*

"Temptations are oft-times right profitable to man, though they be heavy and grievous, for in them a man is meeked, purged and sharply taught . . . Learn to obey, thou dust! learn to meek thyself, thou earth and clay."[1] (To "meek" is an old verb meaning to "humble".)

Our natural thought does not connect meekness with strength. Our natural thought is all wrong there. The truly strong are the gentle, the Strongest of all was the gentlest: "I am gentle and lowly in heart". — Matt. 11. 29 Weym.

As I pondered this word from the Psalm and thought of our Lord's life, always triumphant, never cast down by disappointment, by weariness, by apparent failure, or even by the certainty of suffering swiftly drawing nearer, I wondered if the cause of our cast-down hours is not the hardness of the way (as we are tempted to think it is), but some flaw in the inner spirit which makes it impossible for our God to lift us up. If so, praise Him, it need not remain so : *There is a lifting up.* — Job 22. 29

MARCH 9

Psa. 30. 1 : *I will extol Thee, O Lord: for Thou hast lifted me up, and hast not made my foes to rejoice over me.*

1 Thomas à Kempis.

They would rejoice over us if they could keep us cast down. It would be so evident then that we had a hard Master; that things were not as He had promised they would be; that peace could not be continual; that we could not hope for more than to go on stumbling on our way, depressed and depressing, far, far from being more than conquerors through Him that loved us.

Psa. 3. 2, 3 But *Thou hast lifted me up*, O Lord, *I will extol Thee*, before the gods of this dark world, the mighty powers of sin and of depression, I will sing praise unto Thee. There is no help for him in God—many there be which say that of my soul, but *Thou hast lifted me up* and hast not made my foes to rejoice over me. Thou, O Lord, art a shield for me; my glory, and *the lifter up of mine head*.

MARCH 10

Psa. 19. 10: R.V. mar: *The droppings of the honey-comb.*

This morning I found this marginal reading which was just the word I wanted at the moment. There are times when we cannot read much or even think much. But if we are quiet we shall hear little sweet words dropping into our hearts, "sweeter also than honey and the droppings of the honey-comb." I need not write them; they will be different perhaps to each one of us, but they will be comforting and strengthening too; and we shall go on our way for another day, fed and refreshed.

MARCH 11

Psa. 88. 8: *I am shut up, and I cannot come forth.*
Psa. 86. 4: *Rejoice the soul of Thy servant.*

Very few of you are shut up. For those few who are, these words will be, I think, a great help. The way of joy is the way of release for our spirit, even though the flesh (which is the least part of us) cannot come forth.

But I write the words for you to-day because I think perhaps some are shut up in another way; some difficult thing has to be done, and you do not feel you can do it; you are shut up in discouragement and you think you cannot come forth. Thank

God, you *can*. There is liberty and victory for you. Look up to Him Whose joy is your strength. Pray this prayer, "Rejoice the soul of Thy servant". For you, too, the way of joy is the way of release.

MARCH 12

Before the winds that blow do cease,
   Teach me to dwell within Thy calm;
Before the pain has passed in peace,
   Give me, my God, to sing a psalm,
Let me not lose the chance to prove
The fulness of enabling love.
   O Love of God, do this for me;
   Maintain a constant victory.

Before I leave the desert land
   For meadows of immortal flowers,
Lead me where streams at Thy command
   Flow by the borders of the hours,
That when the thirsty come, I may
Show them the fountains in the way.
   O Love of God, do this for me;
   Maintain a constant victory.

MARCH 13

O Love of God, do this for me,
Maintain a constant victory.

This prayer was written for the ill, and for the very tired. It is so easy to fail when not feeling fit. As I thought of them I also remembered those who, thank God, are not ill and yet can be hard-pressed. Sometimes in the midst of the rush of things, it seems impossible always to be victorious, always to be peaceful, always to be inwardly sweet. Is that not so? Yet that and nothing less is our high calling. So the prayer is really for us all.

O Love of God, do this for me,
Maintain a constant victory.

MARCH 14

Do not fall to a lower level.

These words caught me and held me as I read Westcott's comment on Eph. 5. 17 : "because the days are evil. For this reason do not shew yourselves foolish, but . . ." i.e. "because the danger is great and the need of walking carefully is urgent, . . . do not fall to a lower level". There is always a pull upon us; the great enemy wants to pull our thoughts and words and doings down to a lower level. Our own inner weakness, and sometimes cowardice or love of ease, sides with him; so the pull is tremendous. This week, to-day, perhaps often to-day, we shall feel that pull. By the grace of the Lord let us resist. If we do not resist, the moment we are aware of the pull, we shall fall, just as certainly as the stone thrown up in the air falls to the ground, pulled down by an invisible power.

Psa. 119. 117   Thank God we *can* resist. We can pray in real earnest, "Hold Thou me up, and I shall be safe." In the many choices that will be offered to us we can choose our Lord's. He never chose the easy way.

2 Tim. 4. 16, 17   Suppose the worst happens, suppose all the help we counted on fails us, we can still refuse to fall to a lower level. "No man stood with me, but all men forsook me", wrote Paul the prisoner. "Notwithstanding the Lord stood with me, and strengthened me". The Lord knows all that is behind the "Notwithstanding". He can strengthen us to hold our ground and not to fall to a lower level.

MARCH 15

Eph. 1. 19 : (Rotherham) *According to the energy of the grasp of His might.*

"It's not my grip of Christ, but Christ's grip of me," said an old Scotswoman long ago.

This is a great word for anyone who feels futile, but it is also a great word for us all.

And I think of Paul, so conscious of the surpassing greatness of His power (power whose lightest touch could have snapped his chains) that he could describe that power in heaped-up words of wonder. Yet he was so utterly content in his prison—so unoffended—that his Lord could use him to write deathless letters like this. What a God and what a servant! And He, Who made him what he was, is our God, even ours.

MARCH 16

Take, or receive, *from the hands of God.*

This is Weymouth's note to Eph. 6. 17 about the sword of the Spirit. We all know what it is to be at the end of everything, in deadly fear of defeat in the secret place of the soul. We know, too, what it is to have some word illumined, made vital, made spirit and life to us. As I read that note I saw it thus: Our Father is beside us, and turns over the pages as a father might for his child. He knows our inward need. He knows where to find the word that perfectly fits that need. As we read, He will direct us (whatever the reading be, in our daily sequence, or otherwise), and taking some word in His hands will give it to us. Then if we receive it, holding out our hands for it with longing, it will turn to a sword—"the sword of the Spirit which is the word of God"—and suddenly we shall know that we have "power . . . over all the power of the enemy".

He gives and we receive. And once the sword is in our hands, let us hold it fast. "Take fast hold of instruction; let her not go: keep her; for she is thy life."

Luke 10. 19

Prov. 4. 13

MARCH 17

The same Sword

When I was a little child I used to wish I could touch something that our Lord Jesus touched, or see something that He saw. Then suddenly to my delight I thought, But I *can* see something that He saw. He saw the very same moon and stars that I see. And I used to look at the moon and think, He saw you, He saw those funny marks in your face we call the man in the moon. He looked up to you just as I look up at you to-night. Years afterwards someone gave me a bit of brick and a little slab of marble from Rome. It was wonderful to

Matt. 4. 4

John 6. 63

touch one of them and think, Perhaps the Apostle Paul or one of the martyrs touched this as they passed. But how much more wonderful is it to think that we have, for our own use, the very same sword our Lord used when the devil attacked Him. Westcott says "the word of God" in Eph. 6. 17 means "a definite utterance of God". We know these "definite utterances"—we have the same Book that He had, and we can do as He did. So let us learn the "definite utterances" that they may be ready in our minds; ready for use at the moment of need—our sword which never grows dull and rusty, but is always keen and bright. So once more I say, let us not expect defeat but victory. Let us take fast hold and keep fast hold of our sword, and we shall win in any assault of the enemy. The Lord quicken our expectation.

MARCH 18

Psa. 18. 30 : *As for God, His way is perfect.*

I have been thinking much of this word. We say it, we write it, but the love of God is searching; and it seems to me that all our lives long He is patiently teaching us truly to mean it.

We make plans after much prayer and long waiting. They are on the edge of fulfilment and then something happens to shatter them. If they affected our own life only, it would be easy to say "His way is perfect", but if others must suffer then it is not easy to say those words in sincerity. God knows this. He does not hurry us, but He does wait for us. He waits in His patience till we can look in His face and say—not with a sigh, but with a song—"As for God, His way is perfect". This is victory, nothing less can be called by that shining name.

MARCH 19

Psa. 18. 32 :   *It is God that maketh my way perfect.*
  v. 36 :   *Thou hast enlarged my steps under me, that my feet did not slip.*
  v. 36 :   *Thou shalt make room enough under me for*
  P.B.V.   *to go.*

He maketh my way perfect. Perfect—not easy; high places, steep places, are not easy places, but the hinds' feet are wonderfully prepared to stand on places that would be impossible to most creatures. "He maketh my feet like hinds' feet". Feet that can stand steadily in difficult places, feet that can walk in paths that are like a thread thrown on a precipice, feet that can spring from point to point, not afraid of suddenly having to change direction; all this—and I expect much more—is in the picture David sees and calls "hinds' feet". *v.* 33

And then, lest any one of us should feel afraid of the difficult ways where the hinds go, we have this lovely word : "Thou hast enlarged my steps under me, that my feet did not slip." "Thou shalt make room enough under me for to go". We shall never come to a place where this is not true. There will always somehow be "room for me to go".

MARCH 20

Have you noticed this ? Whatever need or trouble you are in, there is always something to help you in your Bible, if only you go on reading till you come to the word God specially has for you. I have noticed this often. Sometimes the special word is in the portion you would naturally read, or in the Psalms for the day, or in Daily Light, or maybe it is somewhere else; but you must go on till you find it, for it is always somewhere. You will know it the moment you come to it, and it will rest your heart.

Here is a tiny illustration of that : One day I was troubled and anxious about someone. That night I found these words on the page of Daily Light: *I know Whom I have believed,* *and am persuaded that He is able to keep that which I have* *committed unto Him against that day.* And I knew that *this* was His word to me. 2 Tim. 1. 12

MARCH 21

You remember I wrote about the way God speaks to us as we read, meeting us just where we are. I think often it is necessary to go on reading awhile (that is, not stopping at the end of a portion or chapter). If only we go on we shall certainly come to the word that is meant for us. But sometimes for some reason we cannot read for long. In that case we need not be troubled.

He, Who is so near that He knows all about us, knows exactly how things are, and He can meet us in one second of time. It was like that with me this morning, and the word He caused to Mark 10. 49 speak to me like a living voice was : "Be of good comfort, rise; He calleth thee." This word may mean something to me that it will not mean to you; that does not matter. What does matter is that, whatever your need is, He will meet it with a word of Life. Perhaps for some of you these very words will come afresh to-day : "Be of good comfort, rise; He calleth thee." He calleth thee by name. He calleth thee to new service, and for that service He will give new vision, and new power to follow see *v*. 52 Jesus in the way.

MARCH 22

The Trust of the Unexplained

I have been thinking of how many unexplained things there are in life. Our Lord Jesus Who could have explained everything, explained nothing. He said there would be tribulation, but He never said why. Sometimes He spoke of suffering being to the glory of God, but He never said how. All through the Scriptures it is the same. I cannot recall a single explanation of trial. Can you? We are trusted with the Unexplained.

May the Lord our God strengthen us all in every little call upon faith, as well as in every great call, so to live in patience 1 Pet. 1. 7, 8 and steadfastness, that the trial of our faith . . . may be found unto praise and honour and glory at the appearing of Jesus Christ, Whom having not seen, we love.

MARCH 23

Eph. 3. 16-19.

I read these verses in several translations and each separate translation brought out a new wonder of meaning. It is easy Weym. to let such thoughts flow over one—"To be strengthened by His Spirit with power penetrating to your inmost being" was one of the great phrases—but to believe such a thing can really be, *will* really be, is different.

At last, after pondering the mighty words, I went on to verses 20 and 21, and now they seemed to leap up from the page. I understood as never before why Paul wrote them there.

Perhaps some would find it helpful if those last two verses were resolutely not read till the other great words had had time to sink deep into the heart and hold it still in the presence of the Lord. May you have the same experience of sheer wonder that I had.

Now unto Him that is able to do exceeding abundantly above all that we ask or think, according to the power that worketh in us, Unto Him be glory in the church by Christ Jesus, throughout all ages, world without end, Amen.

MARCH 24

Do I believe that God can strengthen us to do things which are humanly speaking quite impossible? It is easy to say, Of course I do. But do I? "A man's right hand is capable of a pull equal to about two thirds of his own weight, but a crab's claw can support a weight equal to thirty times the weight of its own body", so I have read in a book about the Barrier Reef. It sounds impossible.

Sometimes we are asked to do things that seem far too hard for us, to "support a weight" far too heavy for us. But the God with Whom we have to do can do for us what He does for the crab. He can make us strong to do that which looks and feels impossible; He is the God of the Impossible.

MARCH 25

Proverbs 10. 29: *The way of the Lord is strength to the upright.*

If by the grace of God my heart is set on uprightness, then I may count on the fulfilment of this word.

It holds, however one turns it. Is my way beset by temptation? God is faithful, Who will not suffer me to be tempted above that I am able to bear—that way of the Lord, therefore, is strength not weakness or defeat. Do things happen that are shattering to the human in me? "He shall be the   1 Cor. 10. 13

Isa. 33. 6 Darby

stability of thy times." This verse was given to me a few days ago, and I pass it on with joy. There is then no need for us to be shaken and unstable. Is my way clouded? "The Lord shall be a light unto me", so that I can go on in strength.

Never once in Scripture do we find weakness expected in the Christian. There is provision for strength, "the way of the Lord is strength". He Who is our Way is Strength—the joy of the Lord is our strength. May God give it to us to hate the "I can't help it" of the weakling. May He make us strong.

Mic. 7. 8 (margin, by first paragraph)

Neh. 8. 10 (margin, by second paragraph)

MARCH 26

Prov. 24. 10: (Darby.) *If thou losest courage in the day of trouble thy strength is small.*   •

If we want to be among those who are always ready to go the second mile, which often means being quick to see another's trouble, then we must not lose courage in our own. To lose courage is to be "slack". "If thy strength becomes, as it were, pressed together and bowed down by the difficulty, just when it ought to show itself, then it is limited. Thou art a weakling." (Delitzsch.) And no weakling runs the second mile; he does not properly run the first. Luther said, "He is not strong who is not firm in need."

So, let us "be strong in the Lord, and in the power of His might."

Eph. 6. 10 (margin)

MARCH 27

Clouds

This evening the clouds lay low on the mountains, so that sometimes we could hardly see them, and sometimes the stars were nearly all covered. But always, just when it seemed as though the mountains were going to be quite lost in the mist, the higher peaks pushed out, and whereas the dimmer stars were veiled, the brighter ones shone through. Even supposing the clouds had wholly covered the face of the mountains, and not a star had shone through the piled-up masses, the mountains would still have stood steadfast, and the stars would not have ceased to shine.

I thought of this and found it very comforting, simple as it is. Our feelings do not affect God's facts. They may blow up like clouds and cover the eternal things that we do most truly believe. We may not see the shining of the promises, but still they shine; and the strength of the hills that is His also, is not for one moment less because of our human weakness.

Psa. 93. 4

Heaven is no dream. Feelings go and come like clouds, but the hills and the stars abide.

MARCH 28

Luke 9. 34 : *They feared as they entered into the cloud.*

As I read these words, I thought how often we fear as we enter into some cloud of the unknown. The unknown year—or perhaps only the unknown day, can make us fear. Shall we be led through it, always caused to triumph? or shall we fail? Or the cloud may be the sorrow which all of us know so well, the grief (that fills the hour like a cloud) over some well-loved soul that has taken the wrong turn. "They feared as they entered into the cloud."

Luke 9. 34

But "there came a Voice out of the cloud, saying, This is My beloved Son : hear Him", and as we listen we hear. To each heart comes the word it needs most at that moment, and often the first word will be, "Fear thou not", and with the words will come an assurance of His Presence, or a promise of His succour. "And when the Voice was past, Jesus was found alone."

v. 35

v. 36

MARCH 29

Psa. 63. 7 :   *Because Thou hast been my help, there-*
fore in the shadow of Thy wings will I
rejoice.

Song of Songs 2. 3 : *As the apple tree—or any beautiful tree—*
among the trees of the wood, so is my
Beloved among the sons. I sat down under
His shadow with great delight, and His fruit
was sweet to my taste.

So there is joy and nourishment for our souls in the shadow of our Lord. Sometimes we fear as we think of the shadow—

Luke 9. 34

"They feared as they entered into the cloud." But after those three disciples had entered into the shadow of that cloud, they found it so wonderful that they wanted to stay there. Let us not be afraid of shadows. Let us not be afraid of clouds. We often meet Him in thick clouds. The shadow is the shadow of our Beloved. He is very near to the place where His shadow is.

MARCH 30

If the Bible had been written in England, there would not have been nearly so many words about the comfort a shadow can be. But it was written in countries where the heat could be very great, and where great open plains of burning sand make the shadow of a great rock something to be remembered.

Psa. 91. 1

Isa. 49. 2

Isa. 4. 6

There are times for us all when these shadow verses are our greatest comforts; these for example : "He that dwelleth in the secret place of the most High shall abide under the shadow of the Almighty." "In the shadow of His hand hath He hid me". "And there shall be a tabernacle for a shadow in the day-time from the heat, and for a place of refuge, and for a covert from storm and from rain."

MARCH 31

> Shadow and coolness, Lord,
>   Art Thou to me;
> Cloud of my soul, lead on,
>   I follow Thee.
> What though the hot winds blow,
> Fierce heat beats up below?
> Fountains of water flow—
>   Praise, praise to Thee.
>
> Clearness and glory, Lord,
>   Art Thou to me;
> Light of my soul, lead on,
>   I follow Thee.
> All through the moonless night,
> Making its darkness bright,
> Thou art my Heavenly Light—
>   Praise, praise to Thee.

Shadow and shine art Thou,
　Dear Lord, to me;
Pillar of cloud and fire,
　I follow Thee.
What though the way is long,
In Thee my heart is strong,
Thou art my joy, my song—
　Praise, praise to Thee.

APRIL 1

Rom. 6. 4 : *We also should walk in newness of life.*
7. 6 : *That we should serve in newness of spirit.*

I looked up the word "Newness" this morning, and found that Young's Concordance gives it, "Freshness".

"We should . . . walk in *freshness* of life."

"We should serve in *freshness* of spirit."

How very far away such a thought is from the dullness that can fall like a fog; how often in the Psalms we see the soul resolutely fighting through that fog into the sunlight. Never does it, as it were, sit down in dullness. There is always a pressing on into this glorious *freshness* of life and spirit.

In "The Spirit of Discipline" Bishop Paget suggests "that we should, in careful reverence and humility, be trying to know more and more of this power of the Resurrection in the life of the body." We can see it "in the lives of the saints; in their clearness and freedom; their successful resolution not to be brought under the power of the things which domineer over most men;" and he goes on to speak also of others, "born and nurtured in conditions like our own, and yet so splendidly unhindered by the things which keep us back." These words have often helped me to seek that freshness which, like the green leaves on the trees, and all sweet springing things about us now, is a perpetual miracle.

APRIL 2

1 Chron. 6. 32 : *They ministered . . . with singing.*
Col. 3. 16 : *Singing with grace in your hearts to the Lord.*

"I beheld, then, that they all went on till they came to the foot of the hill Difficulty at the bottom of which was a spring . . . Christian now went to the spring, and drank thereof to refresh himself, and then he began to go up the hill". *And he*

48

went up singing. Each day of our lives we begin where Christian began—that is if we have found the spring where we drink and refresh ourselves.

I am believing that some, who have perhaps till now tried to avoid climbing the hill Difficulty, will face it with a new purpose—the purpose to climb. Do not forget the spring, and do not forget the song. *"They ministered . . . with singing."*

Let us climb singing.

APRIL 3

Here is an old note in my Bible which helped me often when I was face to face with the awful powers of heathendom.

Bishop Moule was speaking of Psa. 138. 1, *"Before the gods will I sing praise unto Thee"*. It was David's "glad resolve to sing praise unto His God, not in a clear and open atmosphere, but before the gods, the giant powers which lay behind the giant heathenism of his day. He, as it were, looked them in the face and weighed their strength and force, and though they seemed to suggest the hopelessness of the cause of God, he was not moved." "Before the gods will I sing praise unto Thee."

Some may be up against tremendous temptations. All are surrounded, as David was, by powers which seem to suggest the hopelessness of the cause of God. Try David's way—sing.

APRIL 4

Psa. 89. 1 : P.B.V. *My song shall be alway of the loving-kindness of the Lord.*

O praise the Lord, for it is good
    And pleasant and a joyful thing
To lift the heart, as all men should
    Who have so dear a Lord to sing.

The number of the stars He tells,
    And calls each star by his own name :
No two of all His flowery bells
    Or leaves or grasses are the same.

So individual is His thought
    For all of us, did one let go
The hand of Joy, and sore distraught
    Forget to sing, His heart would know.

From rainbow did a colour float,
    Or did a shining sun burn dim,
That were far less for Him to note
    Than dumbness of a child to Him.

O save from that! Let grateful song
    And jubilance of melody,
And loving merry-makings throng
    The road that leads us home to Thee.

APRIL 5

Luke 19. 28 : R.V. *He went on before, going up to Jerusalem.*
John 11. 55 :   *And many went . . . up to Jerusalem.*

In my Harmony of the Gospels these two sentences follow
closely one after the other.

As I think of you, knowing something of what many of you
are called to endure; knowing, too, that there must be much in
every life of which He only knows; these two sentences come
to me again and again.

So long as we are content to be with the many going up to
Jerusalem (doing the usual religious things in the usual way),
our great enemy cares not one whit. But he is on the alert the
moment we leave the many and follow the One in His so
different way of life, and if we persist, his wrath is aroused.
Then come the stinging arrows of the archers (sharp trials of
flesh or of spirit or both). "The archers have sorely grieved him
and shot at him, and hated him : but his bow abode in strength,
and the arms of his hands were made strong by the hands of the
mighty God of Jacob". So it was with Joseph. So it was with
the Greater than he; so it will be with us. Need we fear? The
Lord give it to us not to fear, but to rejoice.

Gen. 49. 23-24

APRIL 6

Song of Songs 2. 14: *Let Me see thy countenance, let Me hear thy voice.*

As we think of our Lord Jesus going through His last week, meeting at every turn unkind faces and frowning looks and hearing hurting words, I think most of us will be reminded of His longing for something very different. *Let Me see thy countenance, let Me hear thy voice.*

A loving, worshipping countenance, a voice that says only love-words—that refreshes His heart.

> Jesus Redeemer, Saviour of sinners,
> With love and with reverence, we worship Thee.

> Worshipping, praising, Lord, we adore Thee,
> For Thine is the kingdom for ever, Amen.

APRIL 7

The last thing He did before His hands were bound.

Luke 22. 50, 51: *And one of them smote the servant of the high priest, and cut off his right ear. And Jesus answered and said, Suffer ye thus far. And He touched his ear, and healed him.*
John 18. 12 : *Then the band and the captain and officers of the Jews took Jesus, and bound Him.*

The last thing the Lord Jesus did before His hands were bound was to heal.

Have you ever asked yourself, If I knew this was the last thing I should do, what would I do? I have never found the answer to that question. There are so very, very many things that we would want to do for those whom we love, that I do not think we are likely to be able to find the chief one of all these. So the best thing is just to go on simply, doing each thing as it comes as well as we can.

Our Lord Jesus spent much time in healing sick people, and in the natural course of events it happened that the last thing He did with His kind hands was to heal a bad cut. (I wonder how they could have the heart to bind His hands after that.)

1 Pet. 2. 21   In this, as in everything, He left us an example that we should follow in His steps. Do the thing that this next minute, this next hour, brings you, faithfully and lovingly and patiently; and then the last thing you do, before power to do is taken from you (if that should be), will be only the continuation of all that went before.

APRIL 8

John 19. 18 : *And Jesus in the midst.*

Matt. 18. 20   "Where two or three are gathered together in My name, there am I in the midst of them." Perhaps familiarity has dulled our sense of the pure wonder of these words, *There am I in the midst of them.*

The story of the troubled men who had shut the doors for fear of the Jews is familiar, too. But the doors of their hearts

John 20. 19   were not shut, and so Jesus came "and stood *in the midst*, and saith unto them, Peace be unto you." How often we have found comfort in that story.

John 19. 18   In reading yesterday about the two thieves and Jesus *in the midst*, I saw in a new way what we all know. These words, which come between the other two which I have quoted, give us our reason for confidence in the continual Presence of our Lord. It is the Christ of Calvary Who makes vital our gatherings together. How solemn it is to see Him among us as the Crucified.

In the same way it is He Who is our Strong Consolation in hours of fear, and the peace which He gives was won for us through suffering and must surely convey something of its own quality.

APRIL 9

Luke 9. 23 : *If any man will come after Me, let him deny himself, and take up his cross daily and follow Me.*

I think often we accept the cross in theory, but when it comes to practice, we either do not recognize it for what it is, or we recognize it and try to avoid it. This we can always do, for the cross is something that can be taken up or left, just as we choose. It is *not* illness (that comes to all), or bereavement (that also is the common lot of man). It is something *voluntarily* suffered for the sake of the Lord Jesus, some denial of self, that would not be if we were not following Him; often it is something that has shame in it (this, of course, was the earliest connotation of the word), such as the misunderstanding of friends and their blame, when the principles which govern our lives appear foolishness to them. It always has at its core the denial of self and self-love in all its manifestation. Self-choices go down before the call to take up the cross and follow. They fade away and cease to be.

APRIL 10

Gal. 2. 20 : (Weymouth) *I have been crucified with Christ, and it is no longer I that live, but Christ that lives in me.*

Just when we most earnestly desire to live like this, the weary old self seems to come to life again—the "I" that we had trusted was crucified with Christ. It is very disappointing when this happens, and the devil watches not far away, and very quietly and with great subtlety he tries to draw us into hopeless distress and despair. If he can do that he is satisfied, for then we are occupied with ourselves, which is what he wants us to be.

The one and only thing is to look straight off ourselves and our wretched failure, and cry to Him Who is mighty to save. He never refuses that cry; so do not fear. The moment self is recognized, look to Him. Do not be discouraged; He is not discouraged. He Who has begun a good work in us will go on to perfect it. The going on may take time; even so, He will go on till (O blessed "till") we are perfected.

Phil. 1. 6: Weym.

APRIL 11

2 Cor. 1. 8 : (Conybeare.) *Exceedingly pressed down, . . . beyond my strength to bear.*

I was reading this to-day and thinking of how St Paul had long ago forgotten all about that time in Asia where he was so "pressed down", and then I read these words spoken in the 14th century : "Children, I commend you from the bottom of my heart into the captivity of the Cross of our Lord Jesus Christ; that it may be in you, over you, behind you, and before you, lying heavy on you, and yet received by you with free and full acquiescence to the will of God, whatever it may please Him to do with you."

We have much happiness in our lives, and we are meant to be happy and grateful and praiseful; and yet for each one who is fighting the real battle, there are times when the words I have written fit as exactly into our spiritual circumstances as if they had been spoken this morning. It has been so all down the ages. It will be so to the end. But one look at our Lord's face and we shall forget it all.

APRIL 12

2 Cor. 11. 28 : R.V. mar. *Things that come out of course.*

Sometimes things seem to happen contrariwise, on purpose. We are prepared for the usual trials of life, but these are not usual. They are things that come "out of course", and they are the most difficult of all to meet peacefully, and to pass through peacefully. They are most upsetting things, as we sometimes call them, and they often continue to try to upset us.

It is very humbling to go through the list of ordinary things, as apparently they were regarded by the first missionaries— labours, prisons, stripes, stonings, shipwrecks, perils, travails— and then stop and consider these added words, "beside the things that come out of course". What were they? We do not know, but, judging by the things which were not counted as "out of course", they must have been a good deal harder than anything that comes our way.

Is there anything that you do not like and did not expect in your to-day? If so, perhaps these words will help you to meet it with serenity.

APRIL 13

1 Kings 8. 56 : *There hath not failed one word of all His good promise.*

I have found that in times of disappointment of any kind, there is great help in these words. There is the fact. Feelings may say what they will, they cannot touch the eternal fact.

One of His good promises is, "Whatsoever is right I will give you." Another is this : "The Lord will not withhold good things from them that walk in innocence." "No good thing will He withhold", so that the thing that is not given could not have been good for us. He knows what is good. Matt. 20. 4
Psa. 84. 11
LXX

It is just here that faith is tested, sometimes very sharply, and we begin perhaps to distress ourselves over the condition attached to the promise. Is it because of something in me that this good thing—as I believed it to be—is not given? God, Who searcheth the hearts, alone knows our need of the cleansing Blood for motive in prayer, but if by His enabling we will to desire His will, then we may leave all torturing thoughts and rest our hearts on Him. *No good thing will He withhold . . . There hath not failed*—nor ever can fail—*one word of all His good promise.*

APRIL 14

Psa. 107. 35 : *He turneth the wilderness into a standing water, and dry ground into watersprings.*

For the wilderness, His glorious Name be praised; for the dry ground, His glorious Name be praised. For were there no wilderness how could we know the beauty of standing water? And were there no dry ground how could we taste the sweetness of the watersprings? For those for whom is appointed the joyful walk on the hill-tops, there are glorious certainties; it is God that girdeth them with strength, and maketh their way perfect. He maketh their feet like hinds' feet, and setteth them upon their high places. Psa. 18. 32,33

May the Lord enlarge the steps for all on high places, and lead all of us, wherever we walk, to His pools and watersprings.

APRIL 15

I believe that if we are to be and to do for others what God means us to be and to do, we must not let Adoration and Worship slip into the second place, "For it is the central service asked by God of human souls; and its neglect is responsible for

much lack of spiritual depth and power." Perhaps we may find
here the reason why we so often run dry. We do not give time
enough to what makes for depth, and so we are shallow; a
wind, quite a little wind, can ruffle our surface; a little hot sun,
and all the moisture in us evaporates. It should not be so.

This has been our God's word to me afresh this morning and
so I pass it on. Is it not worth-while earnestly to set ourselves
towards this? To-day, if we will hear His voice, to-day, this
morning, if we will draw near to Him, He will draw near to us.
In the hush of that nearness we shall not seek anything for
ourselves, not even help, or light, or comfort; we shall forget
ourselves, "lost in wonder, love and praise."

"Let us draw near hither unto God." "Let us follow on to
know the Lord : we shall find Him ready as the morning." The
morning never disappoints us by not coming, neither does our
loving God.

Psa. 95. 7
Jas. 4. 8

1 Sam. 14. 36
Hos. 6. 3 LXX

APRIL 16

This came in the mail yesterday. It was written by a leper.
His hands are gone, and he writes with a pen tied on to the
stump :

> I would not change one little jot
> Of His dear will for me,
> But in my weakness I would go,
> Entrusting all my load of woe
> To Him Who walks with me.

When any of us feel inclined to grumble about trifles, let us
think of that leper. There is nothing better for our ease-loving
souls than to be made thoroughly ashamed of ourselves.

APRIL 17

Psa. 117. 2
P.B.V.

Prov. 4. 18

Here is a glorious word for you all : *His merciful kindness is
ever more and more towards us.* It reminds me of that other
word about the path shining *more and more.* Satan, fears and
feelings, and the voice of the world, all join together sometimes
in saying just the opposite. But "the word of the Lord" shall
stand. So let us hold fast to that *more and more* and go on our
way rejoicing.

APRIL 18

Eph. 5. 19 : *Singing and making melody in your heart to the Lord.*

Do we sing enough? Are we a singing company? It is written that the singers of the Lord's house were to have their portion given them every day. God takes great care of His singers. Neh. 11. 23

The singers did common work, they were over the business of the house of God. "For it was the king's commandment concerning them, that a certain portion should be for the singers, due for every day." Neh. 11. 23

Change the small k to a capital K, and you have something good, something to be counted upon. Singing people are fed, they "feed on faithfulness." They are strong and glad and always have something to give to others. The world is full of sadness. Let us be a singing company even though we grieve with those who are grieving. It would be a happy thing if, among all the sounds that rise from this poor world just now, our joy might be like the joy of Jerusalem that was heard even afar off—afar off among the people about us—afar off, even up to the gates of Heaven. Psa. 37. 3 R.V. mar. Ezra 3. 11-13

APRIL 19

Eph. 1. 4 : (Weymouth) *He chose us as His own . . . before the creation of the world.*

Before "the morning stars sang together and all the sons of God shouted for joy", He loved me, and "chose me as His own". Therefore to-day every spiritual blessing may be truly mine—the nine-fold fruit of the Spirit, love, joy, peace, patience towards others, kindness, goodness (that sweetness of heart that was Christ's), good faith, meekness, self-restraint—so that in the pressure of life I need never fail. Job. 38. 7 Eph. 1. 3 Gal. 5. 22, 23

And all this is "to the praise of the glory of His grace". Eph. 1. 6

The Lord give us to "possess our possessions." Obad. 17

APRIL 20

Psa. 103. 22 : *Bless the Lord . . . in all places of His dominion.*

Some of the places are what we call dry places. For example, when we read our Bibles and do not find any special life-giving word, we are in one of those places. If, however, then and there, in that very dry place in His dominion, we stop for a moment and look up and love Him and bless Him, we shall find (I believe this for I have proved it) that somehow the dryness has gone; we discover a "brook in the way" and we drink and are refreshed.

Perhaps there is something that we have to do, such as a bit of routine work, but we want it to be quickened by His Spirit and we feel dusty and dead; or we have to see someone whom we have often tried to help, apparently in vain, and we do not seem to have the light of hope in our hearts. Turn the occasion into one of praise. Bless the Lord in *this* place of His dominion. Then the rivers will run in the dry place and it shall be no more dry. For that class or meeting, or whatever it be, there will be the quickening touch of life; it will no longer be a matter of mere routine. A new hope will be born, gift of the God of Hope, and so rivers will run in dry places.

APRIL 21

Psa. 36. 8 : *Abundantly satisfied.*

This is meant to be our word always, however things are. Human happiness depends on circumstances—health, freedom from care, joy of being together, work we love, power to do it, and so on. Divine happiness is quite different. It depends on none of these things. It is written that through much tribulation we enter into the Kingdom of God. Ease of any sort was never promised. It seems to me that we are often called to live a double life : in much tribulation (when we think of the poor world); and yet, in the deepest places of our souls, *abundantly satisfied*—and therefore, in peace ourselves, and able to help others to be peaceful.

Psa. 110. 7

Acts 14. 22

APRIL 22

Here is something I read lately and enjoyed:

> A centipede was happy till
>   One day, a toad in fun
> Said, "Pray, which leg goes after which?"
> Which strained his mind to such a pitch
> He lay distracted in a ditch,
>   Considering how to run.

I think there are a good many toads in the world, and sometimes, not in fun at all but very seriously, they manage "to strain our minds to such a pitch", that instead of going on in simplicity we may very easily find ourselves distracted in a ditch, not running, but only considering how to run.

But this need never be. In one of the loveliest nursery pictures in the Bible, we have our God teaching His little child how to walk, taking it by its arms as one does in teaching babies: "When Israel was a child, then I loved him, . . . I taught Ephraim also to go, taking them by their arms;" it is all there—"With human cords used I to draw them, with the bands of love". So did we learn to walk in our Father's nursery; and now that we are out of the nursery and on the race-course—*looking away* (the only time that word occurs in the New Testament) from toads without and within—let us *run* . . . *looking unto Jesus,* our Faith's Princely-Leader—Perfecter. So shall we run and not be weary, and walk and not faint.

Hos. 11. 1, 3

v. 4 Roth

Heb. 12. 1, 2

APRIL 23

Acts 28. 15:   *Paul . . . thanked God, and took courage.*
Neh. 8. 10, 11: *The joy of the Lord is your strength . . .*
(Rotherham)   *Hush! for the day is holy; and be not grieved.*

Is there any one to-day who is tempted to be cast down about anything? "The joy of the Lord is your strength." Think of all the Niagaras of the world, think of all their white force; so, only immeasurably greater, is the joy of our God; that joy, nothing less, is our strength. "Hush! for the day is holy; and be not grieved." (That was the word of the Levites to the people after Nehemiah had given them the glorious assurance about the joy of the Lord.) "Hush" to the thoughts that would depress, for the day is holy; it is the day that the Lord has made, that we may rejoice and be glad in it. Let us join hands with Paul, and thank God and take courage.

APRIL 24

Neh. 8. 11: (Rotherham) *Hush! for the day is holy.*

Long ago, Samuel Rutherford, writing to one in distress, said, "Command your thoughts to be silent." Can we say "Hush!" to ourselves? Can we command our thoughts? I believe we can. God has given us the power to close the shutter of our minds upon hurtful, weakening thoughts. He has provided all manner of shutters. A book that swings us off ourselves and into another world is a very good shutter; a song set to music; beauty; the dear love of those who love us. Above all, there is this: Look at Calvary. Look steadfastly. Take time to look, and all within you will be hushed, for power streams forth from Calvary. We need never know defeat.

Neh. 8. 15 Roth   And our God is a God of joy. "Forth to the mountains, and bring in branches of olive and branches of oleaster . . ." Oleaster is a tree with fragrant yellow flowers. The booths for that happy feast were to be bright with flowers of joy.

APRIL 25

Rom. 12. 12   One evening two of us were talking of the words *rejoicing in hope*. Everyone agrees that we can do nothing among children unless we are hopeful. A hopeless attitude is fatal. But—this was the enlightening word—we are meant to *rejoice* in hope.

The more one thinks of that word the more it opens out. It is one of the words which are spirit and life. As we thought of it, another word flashed across my mind, but for a moment I wondered, Am I imagining it? One can imagine beautiful words but, unless they or their roots are in the Bible, they do not do much for us. This word, however, *is* in the Bible: *Now*

the God of hope fill you with all joy and peace in believing,   Rom. 15. 13
that ye may abound in hope, through the power of the Holy
Ghost. "All joy and peace in believing". I must have read it
and given it to others scores of times, but how the words of the
Lord can kindle—this word does. I commend it to all who are
tempted to discouragement—which is sure to lead to fret of
spirit—"all joy and peace in believing".

APRIL 26

There are four lines in "Rugby Chapel" which are often
with me. The son is speaking to his father, Dr Arnold of
Rugby :

> If, in the paths of the world,
> Stones might have wounded thy feet,
> Toil or dejection have tried
> Thy spirit, *of that we saw nothing.*

Sometimes we wake feeling "down", and we feel like that
all day long for no reason that we can discover—only it is so.

It is useless to try to feel different; trying does not touch
feelings. It is useless to argue with oneself; feelings elude
arguments. Be patient—feelings are like the mists that cover
the mountains in misty weather. The mists pass; the mountains
abide. Turn to your Father, tell Him you know that He loves
you whether you feel it or not, and that you know that He is
with you whether you feel His presence or not. "I beseech
Thee," said one long ago, "let the power of my Lord be great,   Num. 14. 17
according as Thou hast spoken, saying, . . ." I suggest that you
ask the Holy Spirit to bring some "saying" of His to your mind
that has helped you in the past. That saying wherein He has
caused us to trust, "the same is my comfort in my trouble :   Psa. 119. 49, 50
P.B.V.
for Thy word hath quickened me."

Our Lord can enable us so to live that of our inward "toil
and dejection" others see nothing.

APRIL 27

I have often noticed that if any one, who has been asked to
do a difficult thing for the sake of the Lord Jesus, does it and

does it heartily, that one seems almost at once to gain a new power of joy and a wonderful new liberty. Sometimes a shy reserve that covered the soul like a thin sheet of ice melts, and there is freedom to share things and help others; sometimes a dullness that was there before just disappears. To see it do so is like watching a mist dissolve in sunlight. In my reading this morning I came upon the reason for this happy fact. *Thou hast loved righteousness, and hated iniquity: therefore God, even Thy God, hath anointed Thee with the oil of gladness above Thy fellows.* Our Lord Jesus did the will of His Father with delight, He hated that iniquity which so often tries to dominate us—selfishness, surrender to the easy, and so on. Therefore He was the gladdest of all the sons of men. The same law applies to His followers. Who among us can be counted on for happiness? It is those who never take self into consideration at all. By the grace of the Lord they honestly hate iniquity, even the iniquity of self-pleasing, and delight to do the will of their God. They are the happy ones of a family.

Psa. 45. 8 P.B.V.

APRIL 28

Rev. 5. 6 : *And, lo, . . . a Lamb as it had been slain.*

Weym.

"I saw a Lamb . . . He looked as if He had been offered in sacrifice". We follow a Crucified Saviour. Even in Glory He has not lost the look of one who has been offered in sacrifice.

This cannot mean a sad look, for He was anointed with joy above His fellows, but it must mean something which can only be described by the words, "He looked as if He had been offered in sacrifice".

This was the thought that met me this morning. It should not be quite out of reach of even the youngest of His lovers, though it may take a life-time to begin to understand it. But from Him, Who alone has sounded the depths of this thought, come these most loving words—they meet us just where we are: "I know . . . how thou . . . hast borne, and hast patience, . . . and hast not fainted." "I know . . . you endure patiently, and have borne burdens for My sake and have never grown weary."

Rev. 2. 2, 3

" Weym.

May the Lord make this true of us.

APRIL 29

Rom. 8. 29 : *For whom He did foreknow, He also did pre-
destinate to be conformed to the image of His Son.*

Did you ever feel almost hopeless because it seemed so im-
possible that you would ever be in the least like your Lord?
Lately I have been helped by a footnote to this verse in
Conybeare and Howson's *Life and Epistles of St Paul,* which
refers the reader to 2 Cor. 3. 18. *We are gradually transformed
into the same likeness.* The verb is in the present tense, and
Rotherham and Weymouth have, "are being transformed".
Way goes further, "are hourly being transformed".

So it means patience. It is not the work of a moment. If only
we allow no veils to intervene, this transformation will go on
as steadily as the growth of a plant goes on from hour to hour,
for the Lord says it will. I know how the mind snatches at that
"if". Almost despairingly we feel, Yes, but veils do come
between. I think the honest heart will find peace in this other
word : *The Lord will perfect that which concerneth me.* If we
do not want those veils, He will clear them away. He has given
us power over our wills. If the will be set towards beholding,
looking, reflecting, then our Lord will see to the veils.

Psa. 138. 8

2 Cor. 3. 18
A.V., R.V.

APRIL 30

Psa. 145. 2 : *Every day will I bless Thee; and I will praise
Thy Name for ever and ever.*

Every day—that means *this* day. On some days it is much
easier to bless the Lord and praise Him than on other days, but
there are no exceptions : "This is the day which the Lord hath
made; we will rejoice and be glad in it." Whatever the burdens,
however sharp the conflict, the word is the same.

Psa. 118. 24

It is written of Berber, the Turkish Mongul conqueror of
Northern India, "He marched to conquest as to the light, his
face turned towards the world of spirits." In a very different
sense, so may it be with us :

> I, even I, will sing unto the Lord,
> For ever and for ever the Adored;
> I, even I, though I be dust, will sing
> To Him Who even now is conquering.

MAY 1

How often, Lord, our grateful eyes
    Have seen what Thou hast done,
How often does Thy love surprise
    From dawn to set of sun.

How often has a gracious rain
    On Thine inheritance,
When it was weary, wrought again
    An inward radiance.

Thou Who upon the heavens dost ride,
    What miracle of love
Brings Thee more swiftly to our side
    Than even thought can move?

Our love is like a little pool,
    Thy love is like the sea,
O beautiful, O wonderful,
    How noble Love can be.

MAY 2

Psa. 9. 1, 2 : P.B.V. *I will give thanks unto Thee, O Lord,
with my whole heart: I will speak of all Thy
marvellous works. I will be glad and rejoice
in Thee: yea, my songs will I make of Thy
Name, O Thou most Highest.*

Joys are always on their way to us. They are always
travelling to us through the darkness of the night. There is
never a night when they are not coming. So the Psalm for this
morning should be the word of our heart every morning. It is
Psa. 145. 2   the "Every day" word again. "*Every day* will I bless Thee".

64

If any of you feel, But how can we be happy while we are burdened by the sins and sorrows of the world? I say to you, "O thou enemy, destructions are come to a perpetual end . . . Psa. 9. 6-8 P.B.V. But the Lord shall endure for ever : . . . He shall judge the world in righteousness . . ." The day when that word will be fulfilled is on its way, it is hastening. So in faith and in certainty we rejoice, for sin and sorrow shall not endure for ever, they have an end. "But the Lord shall endure for ever :" Alleluia.

MAY 3

John 14. 27 : *Peace I leave with you, My peace I give unto you: not as the world giveth, give I unto you. Let not your heart be troubled, neither let it be afraid.*

Sometimes we feel courageous. We feel strong enough to say about some new thing we are asked to do,

> "Now bid me run
> And I will strive with things impossible,
> Yea, get the better of them."

Sometimes, however, it is not like that. Then these words come, "Peace I leave with you," peace, not conscious power. But as we go on, power comes to do whatever God wants us to do. First peace— then power. That is always God's way. "Let not your heart be troubled, neither let it be afraid."

MAY 4

John 16. 33 : *That in Me ye might have peace.*

These words have brought peace to me this morning. Sometimes our circumstances are so peaceful, that without knowing it we slip into finding our peace in them. Then something happens to disturb them and our peace is disturbed. Sometimes those about us are so dear that our hearts rest in them, and this is good, but it is not enough, for what if one, in whose love we trust, should disappoint us?

Our Lord did not say, These things [the things of Ch. 16] I have spoken unto you, that in your circumstances ye might have peace; or, These things I have spoken unto you that in the love of others ye might have peace; but He did say, "These things"—things of wonder, joy, sorrow, preparation —"I have spoken unto you, that in Me ye might have peace." "Remember the word that I said unto you, The servant is not greater than his Lord . . . if they have kept My saying they will keep yours also." Is there any surprise of grief that our dear Lord has not foreseen? Is there any wound to love that His love has not suffered? "These things I have spoken unto you, that *in Me ye might have peace*."

John 15. 20

MAY 5

The letters of St Paul are full of prayers. I am going through the prayers of his letter to the Philippians.

Phil. 1. 2

Grace be unto you, and peace, from God our Father, and from the Lord Jesus Christ; grace enough for every need of the day; the blessed Presence your light and joy; peace, and all the repose which the grace of God brings, within you and around you; rest on every side.

There may not always be a feeling of this blessedness. "I found never man so religious nor devout that feeleth not . . . sometime, diminution of fervour." But, thank God, our dry days are always followed sooner or later by good rain. "Tribulation going before is wont to be a token of consolation following."

MAY 6

Phil. 4. 7 : R.V. The peace of God, which passeth all understanding, shall guard your hearts and your thoughts in Christ Jesus.

Peaceful thoughts.

This morning this verse helped me very much. There are so many things happening almost every day which would naturally disturb or distress or cast us down. We all know the refuge of prayer, and here we have the promise, not that we shall be instantly given what we want, but that the peace of God shall guard our hearts and thoughts. So the quietness of peaceful thoughts is the first answer God gives to His needy child, and if our thoughts are peaceful we are peaceful too.

MAY 7

Col. 3. 15 : *Let the peace of God rule in your hearts.*

If we open the shutters in the morning the light will pour in. We do not need to beseech it to pour in. It will pour in if we will let it. If we open the sluice in flood-time the water will flow through. We do not plead with it to flow. It will flow if we will let it.

It is so with the peace of God. It will rule in our hearts if only we will let it. If a heart that is disturbed about anything will "let the peace of God rule" (instead of its own desires), that heart may this very day prove this truth.

> *Let not your heart be troubled:*
> *Let the peace of God rule in your hearts.*

John 14. 1

MAY 8

Psa. 147. 14 : *He maketh peace in thy borders.*

There are many things we should greatly like to do, and there are things that all that is in us *longs* to do, but our borders keep us, as it were, hedged in from those things. We cannot cross our borders. They surround us on every side.

Only He Whose understanding is infinite, as the same Psalm says, knows exactly what these borders are. They are different for every soul, but every soul has them, and to each one the word is the same, He maketh peace in our borders—and making them perfect, the LXX says—so that peacefulness (not fret) fills all the space between.

I think this is a beautiful word.

MAY 9

Isa. 26. 3 : *Thou wilt keep him in perfect peace, whose mind* [thought, imagination] *is stayed on Thee.*

We all love that word. Thought and imagination can paint the most distressing scenes, till we all but see them. If, instead of allowing this, we stay our imagination on the Lord, then

68 EDGES OF HIS WAYS

there is no unrest, no fear, no distress. The peace of God keeps
Phil. 4. 7 — our hearts and minds. That peace passes understanding, but
the heart confides in it.

Psa. 143. 6, 8 — Is there anything troubling me to-day? "I stretch forth my
hands unto Thee, O Lord. Cause me to hear Thy lovingkindness in the morning; for in Thee do I trust."

MAY 10

Isa. 26. 3 : R.V. mar. *A steadfast mind Thou keepest in perfect
peace.*

I was delighted to find this rendering to-day. Much is
happening in the great world and very near us also which
shakes and distresses the mind, filling it with perplexity.

Perhaps something may happen to-day that will be very
disturbing— but "a steadfast mind Thou keepest in perfect
peace." Nothing can take these words out of our Book : nothing
can make them untrue.

MAY 11

Luke 8. 45-48 : *The multitude throng Thee and press Thee
. . . And He said, . . . Go in peace.*

The Revised Version is vivid. "The multitudes press Thee
and crush Thee." Many know that crushed feeling. I think our
Lord must have thought of how often His followers would be
2 Cor. 1. 8 — "pressed out of measure, above strength," as one of them said,
because of the throng of things, and because power had gone
out of them; and so He allowed this lovely story to be told.
Thronged, pressed, crushed, tired—for a man is tired when in
some special way power has gone forth from him, and as He
was man as well as God He must have been tired then—yet He
was so peaceful that He could bring peace to the one who was
fearing and trembling.

The more one ponders such a story, the more one sees in it,
and the more one longs to live that life of victory over circumstances, the life which, though outwardly crowded and crushed,
is yet overflowing with peace.

May the peace of our dear Lord fill every hour with peace
to-day.

MAY 12

Mark 5. 36 : *But Jesus, not heeding the word spoken.* . . .
R.V.

He heard, but He took no notice. "Who is blind, but My
Servant? or deaf, as My Messenger that I sent? Seeing many
things, but Thou observest not". Have we learned to follow
Him there? How often one, who has truly asked for the gift of
peace, finds peace upset by something that someone has said.
"Not heeding the word spoken," to be deaf to it, to go on as if
one had not heard it—this is something not all of us find easy.

May the Lord give us this holy deafness and blindness,
where the word spoken or the thing done is hindering the
perfect fulfilment of His will. "They say. What say they? Let
them say." These words were carved over the door of an old
monastery. The Lord carve them upon our memories.

Isa. 42, 19, 20

MAY 13

What the ticking of the clock said.

One night I was awake. All was quiet, except for the ticking
of the clock; I was in trouble about something and could not
forget the trouble. Presently the steady tick-tock, tick-tock
began to sound like words:

> Commit your care, commit your care,
> For I am here, and I am there.
> Commit, commit, and do not fear,
> For they are dear and you are dear.

"There" of course was the place I was thinking of, and
"they" were the people I was thinking of. Last night the clock
spoke in different words:

> Where is your care? Where is your care?
> You cannot find it anywhere,
> You cannot find it anywhere.
> I heard your prayer, I heard your prayer.

It was quite true. The care had gone. I could not find it
anywhere.

I wonder if any of you who have burdens will let the ticking of the clock take words for you? I tell you of how it took words for me, because I have so often found that little things that help me can help others too.

MAY 14

John 14. 27 : *Peace I leave with you, My peace I give unto you.*

It has come to me afresh that peace and suffering are closely linked together in the New Testament. The words quoted lead on to Gethsemane and Calvary.

A letter, which begins with persecution and tribulation, and prays that those who read it might be counted worthy of the Kingdom of God for which they suffer, ends with "Now the Lord of peace Himself give you peace at all times in all ways."

2 Thess. 3. 16
R.V.

We do not know what the Thessalonians had to endure; we only know that it was a thousand times more than anything we have ever experienced, for the New Testament words always contain the most, not the least, possible meaning, so a great scholar has said. Beside these immense trials what are ours? They may seem large to us for the moment, and perhaps no one knows of them. That does not matter, for He Who loves best of all knows all about that, and He says, "My peace I give unto you". His peace is not the easy, natural peace of the level road. It is the peace of the steep and difficult mountain climb.

Make us Thy mountaineers; . . .
That undefeated we may climb the hill
As seeing Him Who is invisible.

MAY 15

Hebrews 10. 36 : *Ye have need of patience.*
Phil. 4. 19 :   *My God shall supply all your need.*

I never put these two verses together until this morning. Even little children know what it is to be tempted to be impatient, and all through our lives we are tempted in this way. Perhaps there is nothing we need more than patience—

patience when we do not understand things or when they cannot be explained; patience when things do not turn out as we hoped they would; patience with people; patience with ourselves; and patience in the midst of disturbing circumstances.

We have need of patience . . . Our God shall supply all our need.

MAY 16

Luke 8. 15 : *And bring forth fruit with patience.*

The first meaning is the one of which we have often thought; but the words of our Lord are rich, and another meaning came out of these words one evening. It seemed to me that we are all continually being given chances to bring forth fruit with patience. Those who are ill long to be fit and in full work; and yet to long impatiently only hinders and depresses, whereas in patience is continued fruitfulness. All soul-winners and soul-tenders are given this same opportunity as they give themselves to help others, for souls cannot be hustled. When you feel as if you had come to the end of your patience do not scourge yourself. Patience never came that way. Go to the One Who is the God of patience and consolation, and He will renew you in patience.   Rom. 15. 5

MAY 17

Ecclus. 17. 24 : *He comforteth them that are losing patience.*

He is accustomed to do this, so accustomed to do it that He has taken for one of His beautiful names, *The God of Patience.* It is good to know that He never tires of comforting them that are losing patience, and when He comforts them, all is well; they go on—even unto the end.   Rom. 15. 5

. . .   He comforteth
Them that are losing patience. 'Tis His way :
But none can write the words they hear Him say
For men to read, only they know He saith
Sweet words, and comforteth.

MAY 18

Rom. 15. 5 : *The God of Patience.*

When I looked up the name, *the God of Patience,* I found something that may help those who find it difficult to be always with others, never alone. (The slaves in the Roman houses must have found it exceedingly difficult; perhaps that is why these words were written to them.) "Now the God of patience and consolation grant you to be like-minded one toward another according to Christ Jesus." The end of that was not just that they might have a happy time together—though they certainly would have that, for love is the most "happyfying" thing in all the world—but that with one mind and one mouth they might *v. 6* glorify their God.

v. 7 "Wherefore receive ye one another [go more than half-way to meet one another, be tender to one another], as Christ also received us".

May the God of Patience grant us to be like-minded.

MAY 19

God of patience and endurance,
    Steadfast as the steadfast stars
Stands Thy promise, Thine assurance
    Unto Thine ambassadors;
I, thy God, will strengthen thee,
Where I am, there thou shalt be.

Lord, we would endure, O sift us
    Clear of weakness, make us strong;
Lord, we would endure, O lift us
    Into joy and conquering song;
Cause us in Thy peace to dwell
Seeing the Invisible.

Let us welcome all life's weather
    Whatsoever it may be,
And, or singly, or together,
    Find our heart's delight in Thee,
Our Redeemer, our Adored,
Lover and belovèd Lord.

MAY 20

Eccles. 2. 26 : R.V. *To the man that pleaseth Him God giveth wisdom, and knowledge, and joy.*

It was that "and joy" that caught my attention last night, and I want to pass it on. Wisdom and knowledge are necessities if we are to do our work properly, but joy seems to me such a kind and lovely extra (like the scent of a flower); and then there is this, "I know that, whatsoever God doeth, it shall be for ever: nothing can be put to it, nor any thing taken from it". Nothing that happens (if only it comes to us in the line of His will) can take anything from the joy that does not depend on circumstances but on our God Himself. If only we are kept by His power from anything that grieves the Spirit, it will be so always, "for to the man that pleaseth Him God giveth . . . joy." Ch. 3. 14

MAY 21

Jas. 1. 2 : *Count it all joy.*

It is a tremendous command. I wonder if any of you will find it as searching as I do. "Count it all joy when ye fall into divers temptations". Endure, yes, by God's grace we can rise to that; but *count it all joy?* That is different.

Then I read *v.* 1 : "James, bond-slave of God and of the Lord Jesus Christ". There was a time when James was far from calling the One Who was his Brother, "the *Lord* Jesus *Christ*"; or himself, His slave. He must many a time have seen that sinless Brother meet divers temptations. Is this word about a greater victory of spirit over flesh than just endurance would be, reminiscent of something seen in the home at Nazareth, or when His kinsmen (perhaps among them James himself) said, "He is beside Himself"—worse than foolish, mad? Greek

Mark 3. 21
mar.

He has left us "an example that we should follow His steps". Lord, strengthen us to follow; it is not in us to "count it all joy"—Lord, enable us; hold us to the highest. 1 Pet. 2. 21

MAY 22

Deut. 28. 47, 48 : *Because thou servedst not the Lord thy God with joyfulness, and with gladness of heart, for the abundance of all things; therefore shalt thou serve thine enemies which the Lord shall send against thee, in hunger, and in thirst, and in nakedness, and in want of all things.*

Jer. 31. 3

And He, Who in another place says that He draws us with lovingkindness, says now that He shall put a yoke of iron upon our neck.

So dullness of spirit is sin; there is no way out of that conclusion. I think we sometimes call it by other names; "sensitiveness" is one of its pet names; and so we take things by the wrong handle, turn a dull face instead of a glad one on the rough and smooth of life, depress others and make it harder for them to be good. May the Lord deliver us from all this, and show us this dullness of spirit for what it is—ungratefulness,

2 Cor. 11. 28

selfishness, sin. There will be sorrow; the care that cometh daily; battle wounds may knock us out; but we need never go under in spirit. May He keep us all and make us a joyful company, each one of us like that servant of His (the mother of Bishop Moule) "whose feet brought light into a room". Let us all ask for that blessed gift, "joyfulness and gladness of heart for the abundance of all things".

MAY 23

Psa. 105. 41 : *He opened the rock, and the waters gushed out; they ran in the dry places like a river.*

Have any of us any dry places? They may be out of sight of even loving eyes. We may be ashamed to think there are such places when we have so much to fill our lives with song and praise, and yet there they are, dry places of longings, weariness, disappointment, difficulty of any sort, failure.

Oh, blessed be the love of God; "the waters . . . ran in the dry places like a river." There is no need to go on in dryness.

Isa. 51. 3

"For the Lord shall comfort Zion : He will comfort all her waste places; and He will make her wilderness like Eden, and her desert like the garden of the Lord; joy and gladness shall be found therein, thanksgiving and the voice of melody."

MAY 24

Psa. 37. 5 : (Kay) *Roll thy way upon the Lord.*

Way means a trodden path, the journey of life, to-day's life. Often when we cannot lift a thing we can roll it, and so the Hebrew uses this simple word which we can so easily understand. Roll everything that concerns thee upon the Lord. Roll it again, no matter how many times you did so before, and then rest, "assure thyself in Him, and He, He Himself, will work." French Version Darby

MAY 25

Luke 22. 32 : *But I have prayed for thee, that thy faith fail not.*

Our Lord Jesus prayed for Peter that his faith might not fail, and within a few hours his faith did fail.

The more we think of those last hours of our Lord just before Calvary, the more we see every kind of trial compressed into them. It was not only that His cup was filled to overflowing with suffering, but that every variety of suffering was there. It is easy to escape from the intolerable sense of such suffering by saying, He was God; for example, where Peter was concerned we may say that He saw across to the victory that would be given. But we know, though we cannot understand it, that He was man, too, and the word in Hebrews says that He suffered being tempted; to suffer means to endure or experience pain, so there is no escape by that door. Heb. 2. 18

Is there one for whom we are praying who seems to be unhelped by that prayer? Are we suffering, enduring, experiencing the bitterness of disappointment? Our dear Lord has been this way before. We shall find Him there. He Who "turned, and looked upon Peter" will give to us, will maintain in us, His own eternal tenderness of spirit, the love that cannot be tired out of loving, the patience that will not let go. Luke 22. 61

MAY 26

1 Cor. 10. 13 : *God is faithful, Who will not suffer you to be tempted above that ye are able.*

The pressure of temptation is measured by One Who knows what the substance to be tested can stand. The maker of glass would not subject his glass to a weight of 20 tons per sq. inch.

1 Pet. 4. 19

Here lies our comfort. We commit our souls "as unto a faithful Creator." Sometimes we feel so ashamed of finding something heavy which, after all, is only a little weight, that we miss our comfort. Whether it be so tiny that others cannot see why it should be a trouble at all, or whether it be a huge thing like a twenty ton weight, He knows all about it. He measured its weight before He put it upon us.

And there is more in this. Sometimes we are tempted to feel that even though the pressure would be nothing to another who

Psa. 103. 14

is stronger, it is too much for us. But it never is : "He knoweth our frame; He remembereth that we are dust." The temptation to yield and do what the flesh would naturally do, is meant to offer us an opportunity for endurance, and for the exercise of

Rev. 13. 10

faith. This "is the patience and the faith of the saints."

MAY 27

Psa. 42. 6 : *The Hill Mizar*

Did you ever feel that you had nothing great enough to be called a trouble, and yet you very much needed help? I have been finding much encouragement in the hill Mizar. For Mizar means littleness—the little hill. The land of Jordan was a place where great floods (the swelling of Jordan) might terrify the soul, and the land of the Hermonites was a place of lions and leopards; but Mizar was only a little hill : and yet the word is, I will "remember Thee from . . . the hill Mizar", *from the little hill.*

So just where we are, from the place of our little trial, little pain, little difficulty, little temptation (if temptation can ever be little), let us remember our God. Relief will surely come, and

v. 8

victory and peace; for "the Lord will command His loving-kindness", even to us in our little hill.

MAY 28

1 Pet. 1. 7 : *The trial of your faith, being much more precious than of gold . . . though it be tried with fire.*

Every trial is a trust. The Oxford Dictionary gives the history of the word "trial" from 1526, onward. One early use was, "the action of testing or putting to the proof the fitness, truth, strength or other quality of anything."

By 1554 it meant, "that which puts to the test; especially a painful test of one's endurance, patience, or faith; hence affliction, trouble, misfortune."

1608 gives a new use of the word. It will give all who think food for thought. "Something that serves as an example or proof of a manufacture or material, the skill of an operator, and especially in pottery manufacture, a piece of clay, or the like, by which the progress of the firing process may be judged, a trial-piece."

"But now, O Lord, Thou art our Father; we are the clay, and Thou our Potter;" Thou dost trust us to be Thy trial-piece.

Isa. 64. 8

MAY 29

I expect some of us felt, I am not much of a trial-piece. I have often failed my Lord. Some of us have watched an Indian potter at work. We have seen the clay "marred in the hand of the potter," but we have never seen it thrown away as useless. Always "he made it again another vessel as it seemed good to the potter to make it. Cannot I do with you as this potter? saith the Lord."

Jer. 18. 4, 6

There is a difference between clay in the hands of the potter and clay in the fire. If the trial-piece cracks, it is the end of it, so far as the earthly potter is concerned; but, thank God, not so when He is the Potter. He is the God of the Impossible. So if to any one the devil of discouragement is whispering discouraging lies, do not listen to them. Even if we have failed in some supreme test, our God has not done with us. He deals wondrously with us; as Joel says, "Praise the name of the Lord your God, that hath dealt wondrously with you."

Joel 2. 26

MAY 30

This is from a note sent to me, illustrating very beautifully the story of one who, watching a potter, thought that he could make a pot on the wheel, and tried, but failed:

Then the potter said, "sit down, you can make a pot." "That I cannot do, as you see by what I have already done", I replied. "Sit down", he insisted. I did so. Then, sitting behind me, he put his arms over my arms, his hands over mine, his fingers over my fingers. The wheel began to spin. "Do not allow your fingers to resist mine", he advised, and I obeyed. There under my fingers, to my astonishment grew a beautiful vessel. The wheel stopped and my friend said, "Behold your pot." "Not mine", I said. "Look on your hands, there is clay on your fingers, so they touched the clay, for there is nothing on my hand. Whose hand touches the vessel, that hand makes the pot", the potter said and smiled. Heb. 13. 20, 21 "Now the God of peace . . . make you perfect in every good work to do His will, working in you that which is wellpleasing in His sight."

MAY 31

YEA

Heb. 13. 8 : R.V. *Jesus Christ is the same yesterday and to-day, yea and for ever.*

I had forgotten that this little word was in this verse till I came upon it a few days ago. I think it must have been put there for the special comfort of the specially tempted.

We do want to be whole-hearted for our Lord. We do want to please Him perfectly. For to-day we can trust and not be afraid, but what about to-morrow?

So the blessed Spirit Who helpeth our infirmities caused this most reassuring of little words to be put into that great statement: "Jesus Christ is the same yesterday and to-day, yea and for ever." And He "Himself hath said, I will in no wise fail thee, neither will I in any wise forsake thee. So that with good courage we say, The Lord is my helper; I will not fear: what shall man [or devil or my own weak heart] do unto me?" With me is One Who is the same yesterday and to-day, yea and for ever.

Heb. 13. 5, 6: R.V.

JUNE 1

Psa. 103. 21 : *Bless ye the Lord, . . . ye ministers of His, that do His pleasure.*

This is a perfect word for a new month.

We have nothing to do but that happiest of all things, the pleasure of God. "Now the God of peace . . . make you perfect in every good work to do His will, working in you that which is wellpleasing in His sight." Shall we take these three words from Delitzsch's translation as our motto for the month. "Doing His pleasure"?

Heb. 13. 20, 21

Is this not a joyful thought? I have nothing to do all day long but to please my Lord Jesus, "doing His pleasure".

JUNE 2

Psa. 143. 10 : P.B.V. *Teach me to do the thing that pleaseth Thee.*

I want this note to help even the youngest who is in earnest to live a holy life. So I will write something so simple that at first reading it will seem hardly worth writing at all.

There are two prayers, one of which we are constantly praying, sometimes in words, sometimes in thoughts, always in actions. One is, "Teach me to do the thing that pleaseth *Thee*;" the other is, "Lord, let me do the thing that pleaseth *me*." If we are honest with our God He will show us which of these two prayers we habitually use. Some use the first in the morning, and the second all through the day; for such, the second is the habit of the soul. Some vary between the two, and that leads to an up-and-down life. Some are growing more and more into the first as an all-day prayer, and their lives are growing stronger and gladder, more equable, more dependable, and much more peaceful.

79

I do not think anything worth having in the spiritual world is easily attained, there is no short-cut to holiness. But there can be a true, humble, loving choice of the soul, and that choice, becoming a habit, will lead it into peace.

JUNE 3

Deut. 2. 3 : *Ye have compassed this mountain long enough.*

There is a mountain which, when I find myself compassing it, I call by this name, Discontent with the ways of God. It has other names which sound nicer, but I think this name strips it of all pretence.

How can we know if we are compassing that mountain? Do we fit anywhere into this sentence from the "Imitation"? "Many privily seek themselves in things that they do, and wot not thereof. It seemeth them also that they stand in their good peace when all things fall after their will and their feeling. And if it fall otherwise than they desire, they are soon moved and sorry." If we find ourselves there, then we may know that we are compassing that mountain. But we need not compass it for one hour longer. "Ye have compassed this mountain long enough." It is a trumpet-note word. We are called to be soldiers. Soldiers obey the call of the trumpet. Let us obey.

JUNE 4

Heb. 10. 36 : *Ye have need of patience [steadfast endurance], that, after ye have done the will of God, ye might receive the promise.*

This verse made me think of how continually our Lord
John 14. 21   makes obedience the test of love: "He that hath My commandments, and keepeth them, he it is that loveth Me." I was thinking, too, of how each act of obedience opens a window in Heaven, and light pours through upon the soul that obeys, and it walks on in that Heavenly light; whereas, just as certainly, the least disobedience shuts the window. No more light can come through. Then I came on this verse in Hebrews, which makes patience the link between obedience and receiving in their fulness the promises of God.

How does this bear upon our life to-day? Well, first I think
that obedience is taken for granted (a disobedient child is not
even contemplated). Can God take my obedience for granted?
If He cannot, there can be only one reason; "He that hath My
commandments, and keepeth them, *he it is that loveth Me.*"
If I disobey, it must be because I love someone else more. Who?
But if that point has been passed, and the soul loves its Lord
better than itself, and some word of His has been obeyed, or
some urging in prayer yielded to, then may come the need of
steadfast endurance. I think it often does. Lord, give to us all
to obey and to endure, that even we may receive, for the
enriching of other lives, Thy "exceeding great and precious   2 Pet. 1. 4
promises".

JUNE 5

Heb. 10. 38, 39 : *If any man draw back* [*shrink back*] . . .
              *But we are not of them who draw back unto
              perdition.*

We must all have read these words often; but did their
startling meaning break full upon us? To draw back, to shrink
back, is to perish. We only live as we go on.
    It is a very solemn thing. God shows us a truth in His Word.
He makes His will clear to us. Some command, as it were,
speaks aloud in our souls, and we know it is not man's voice but
God's; or we see our Lord's wish for us in such a chapter as
1 Cor. 13, or in Col. 3. 13, or Matt. 5, or anywhere else; then
what happens? Either we walk on towards it, or we shrink
back from it. We cannot stand still and mark time. It must be
either forward or back—*to draw back is to perish.*
    I do feel that this is the word given to me to-day to write.
It came to me myself first. It is always possible to shrink back,
but thank God, it is never necessary. "I can . . . through   Phil. 4. 13
Christ" must be for ever true.
    But what if we have shrunk back? There was one who did,
and his Lord turned and looked upon him, and he never shrank   Luke 22. 61
back again. It was he who wrote of the "exceeding great and   2 Pet. 1. 4
precious promises" given, so that we may share "in the very
nature of God." Christ did not shrink back.   Weym.

JUNE 6

Phil. 2. 13 : *For it is God Which worketh in you both to will and to do of His good pleasure.*

Do any of you feel the need of renewing in will-power? Satan loves to attack our wills. This is a great word for that—it came with fresh force this morning : this is Dr Way's rendering: "You have not to do it in your unaided strength: it is God Who is all the while supplying the impulse, giving you the power to resolve, the strength to perform, the execution of His good-pleasure."

> With Heavenly power endue us,
> With Heavenly love fulfil,
> Perform in us Thy pleasure,
> Teach us to do Thy will.

JUNE 7

Exod. 3. 5 : *Put off thy shoes from off thy feet, for the place whereon thou standest is holy ground.*

There are two Heavenly words, one a prayer and the other an assurance, which seem to have been written for those of us who feel that we have not "put off our shoes" as we should have done.

Psa. 86. 11
Psa. 130. 3, 4

"Oh, knit my heart unto Thee that I may fear [reverence] Thy Name"—*Thy Name.* "If Thou, Lord, shouldest mark iniquities, O Lord, who shall stand? But there is forgiveness with Thee, that Thou mayest be feared [reverenced]."

Psa. 130. 3, 4
P.B.V.

Unite my heart, knit my heart—there is the prayer for us. But the chief thought with me to-day is the joy of this: "If Thou, Lord, wilt be extreme to mark what is done amiss : O Lord, who may abide it? For there is mercy with Thee : therefore shalt Thou be feared."

What if He were "extreme"? But He is not. "Oh, what a Redeemer is Jesus my Saviour!"

> From Him, Who loves me now so well,
> What power my soul shall sever?
> Shall life, or death, or earth, or hell?
> No; I am His for ever.

J. G. Small

JUNE 8

Judges 15. 19 : *En-hakkore, the well of him that cried.*

Samson was hot and tired and thirsty there on the hill, thereafter known as The lifting up of the jaw-bone, or The casting away of the jaw-bone, or for short, The jaw. There was, I suppose, water underground, a hidden spring, as there is in so many hills, but Samson did not see it, did not know it was there. "He was sore athirst, and called on the Lord, and said, Thou hast given this great deliverance into the hand of Thy servant: and now shall I die for thirst? . . . But God clave an hollow place that was in the jaw, and there came water thereout; and when he had drunk, his spirit came again, and he revived". And he gave the place its beautiful name, *The well of him that cried.* *v.* 18 *v.* 19

Have you ever been strengthened to win a victory perhaps over some inward foe, and have you suddenly found yourself tired out and sore athirst? Quite close, just where you are, there is water. Call, and the Lord will cause it to flow for you; some word of life will come to mind, some line of a hymn, some thought of peace, and your spirit will come again and you will be revived.

JUNE 9

Phil. 1. 6 : *Being confident of this very thing, that He Which hath begun a good work in you will perform it until the day of Jesus Christ.*

Is not this a perfect word? Bishop Moule says the Greek word translated "will perform it" means "will evermore put His finishing touches to it". Think of the fingers that made the blue of the kingfisher's wings, and every other lovely thing on earth, putting finishing touches to you and to me to-day. Is there one of us who would hinder Him?

These finishing touches often come through the sweet joys of life, but they come, too, through the tiny trials, the little disappointments, the small things we hardly like to speak about, and yet which are very real to us. Let us think of them as the touches of His fingers—the finishing touches.

JUNE 10

Psa. 66. 20 : (Rotherham) *Blessed be God, Who hath not turned away my prayer, nor His own lovingkindness from me.*

This morning these words were balm to me. The day may bring many strange things to us, perplexing or painful or disappointing; but this stands strong—our prayer has not been turned away, nor His lovingkindness.

It flows to us still like a river, and over us like the waves of the sea, and soothes and refreshes like music. I have found it a help and a strength to give this great truth time to sink into the mind. It quiets the spirit and comforts it and brings back songs.

> Lover of souls, Thee have I heard,
>   Thee will I sing, for sing I must;
> Thy good and comfortable word
>   Hath raised my spirit from the dust.

JUNE 11

1 Pet. 4. 12 : *Beloved, think it not strange concerning the fiery trial which is to try you . . .*

Jas. 1. 2 : *My brethren, count it all joy when ye fall into divers temptations . . .*

Weym.

"Think it not strange" goes a long way, but "Count it all joy" goes much further. "Reckon it nothing but joy, my brethren, whenever you find yourselves hedged in by various trials." Is it not an amazing word? I am constantly struck by the way the New Testament writers absolutely refuse the natural human point of view where trial is concerned (and of course all other matters also). They have caught the vision of their Master. They talk as He talked, for they think as He thought. "Think through me, thoughts of God".

Let us ask that we may rise to prayer on these lines for one another. I so often find myself praying for relief from trial for those who are being tried, and I think, within limits, we may do this, for we are all our Father's little children and He understands. But we do need to rise to the "Count it all joy" view.

We need to look beyond the present, through the present, to the things that are not seen, and in our prayers for one another, and in our faith for one another, to rise to the highest.

JUNE 12

Heb. 3. 1 : (Weymouth) *Fix your thoughts on Jesus.*

To read slowly and ponder Heb. 2. 18 and 3. 1 is an immense help towards this kind of thinking and this kind of praying. All the versions are beautiful : "For in that He Himself hath suffered being tempted, He is able to succour them that are tempted. Wherefore consider Christ Jesus". "For inasmuch as He has Himself felt the pain of temptation and trial, He is also able instantly to help those who are tempted and tried. Therefore fix your thoughts on Jesus . . . Whose followers we profess to be." Weym.

It is the "For" and the "Inasmuch" that lift us up here. Apart altogether from the comfort that lies on the surface of these wonderful words about our dear Lord and his power instantly to help us, because He knows all there is to know of the pain of temptation and trial, there is this : if we are His followers we, too, shall find that every experience of temptation and trial will turn to power to help others. Therefore "count it all joy", and that it may be so, "Fix your thoughts on Jesus . . . Whose followers we profess to be."

JUNE 13

Sometimes our thoughts will not stay "fixed", we cannot explain why. Before we know it, we find we have drifted back to thoughts of ourselves, or of others, or of places, or things, of anything, indeed, but of Him Who is deepest down our greatest longing—"Thou, O Lord God, art the thing that I long for". Psa. 71. 4
P.B.V. I expect the wise could tell of many ways of help. I will tell of the simplest I know. You have tried reproaching yourselves, Why can I not do better than this? Try "singing to yourselves" instead. Try what some beloved little hymn or song or psalm will do. Psalm 71. 23 tells us just what happens then : "My lips shall greatly rejoice when I sing unto Thee; and my soul which Thou hast redeemed." A.V.

For He has delivered us. He delivered us the moment we looked to Him, and when we sing to ourselves in this way, we are really singing to Him, our dear Deliverer, and before we know it the gloom has passed, we are out in the sunshine again.

JUNE 14

Eph. 5. 19 : *Speaking to yourselves in psalms and hymns and spiritual songs, singing and making melody in your heart to the Lord.*

The reason why singing is such a splendid shield against the fiery darts of the devil is that it greatly helps us to forget him, and he cannot endure being forgotten. He likes us to be occupied with him, with what he is doing (our temptations), with his victories (our falls), with anything but our glorious Lord. So sing. Never be afraid of singing too much. We are much more likely to sing too little.

There are times, however, when we cannot sing aloud. This verse covers that inward singing that so often lifts the heart Heavenward. God make us a singing company.

JUNE 15

2 Cor. 4. 1 : (Conybeare) *"Having this ministration, I discharge it with no faint-hearted fears.*

I read these words this morning, and then I read the previous verses, and they explain how it can be possible to discharge the ministry with no faint-hearted fears. "But we all, with open face beholding as in a glass the glory of the Lord, are changed into the same image from glory to glory, even as by the Spirit of the Lord." "All" means all. It is easy to think of the silver surface of a lake reflecting the glory of the sun; but the merest scrap of tin will reflect, if only it be clean, and nothing comes between it and the sky. So that "all" includes the most tinny of us, and the only thing that matters is that we should be clean, and that nothing should come between us and our Heavenly Sun. We need never be fainthearted.

JUNE 16

1 Tim. 6. 11 : (Conybeare) *But thou, O man of God, follow
. . . steadfastness* (and the note to the
word steadfastness is, "steadfast endurance under persecution").

I have been thinking of the persecution of circumstances.
The body can be persecuted by pain, weariness, lack of strength
to do, and so on. The spirit can be persecuted by disappointment, rending of many kinds, such as the particular kind our
Lord described in Matt. 7. 6. Those who have given their
pearls—pearls of love, every kind of pearl they had to give—
and have then met ingratitude and perhaps untruth, know
what these words mean. But come what may, "O man of God
[O woman of God], follow steadfastness". No persecution,
whether it be of body or of spirit, need ever conquer us. We are
called to fight the good fight of faith. If we *saw* the victorious
issue of the fight, it would not be a fight of faith. If we *saw* the
end of the road clearly and the reason why we are being led
along this particular road, we would not walk by faith, but by
sight. Again and again the emphasis is on faith.

*Lord, increase our faith that we may follow steadfastness—
even unto the end.*

JUNE 17

Matt. 15. 25 : R.V. *But she came and worshipped Him.*

Her prayer had met first silence, and then a perplexing
answer, for she must have heard our Lord Jesus' words to His
disciples, and she would know what they meant. It was all
perplexity then, and disappointment. *But* she came and worshipped. (The Revised Version brings out the force a little more
than the Authorized, so I follow it here.)

These words spoke to my heart to-day. Sometimes our
prayer does not at once meet with the response we expected,
and the temptation then is to discouragement. "But she came
and worshipped".

May the Lord work in us both to will and to do, so that
conquering the natural inclination of our weak hearts, we shall

88 EDGES OF HIS WAYS

turn our disappointments to causes and occasions for worship. Worship may lead on to renewed intercession, as it did in this blessed story, but first let there be worship, the adoration of the lover, the quietness of faith.

JUNE 18

Exod. 30. 35 : R.V. *Thou shalt make of it incense, a perfume . . . seasoned with salt.*

marginaliaHeb. 4. 12

I am sure you all know what it is to find something take life as you read it, and become quick and powerful, sharper than any two-edged sword, piercing, discerning. A word came to me in that way, as I read it in the Revised Version. Incense (which typifies prayer) was to be *salted, seasoned with salt.*

marginaliaLev. 2. 13

Offerings, of course, had to be salted : "With all thine offerings thou shalt offer salt"—salt which is the symbol of truth, incorruptibility, purity. And this word goes deep, it is truly a discerner of the thoughts and intents of the heart. But the other, it seems to me, goes even deeper. It deals with our prayers, our wishes spoken into the ear of God, our praise, too, and our worship said or sung. It is a searching word.

We can escape it if we will. We can say, It is too high for me, too searching for me; or we can take the words of Psalm 141. 2 and say to our God Who seeth the heart, "Let my prayer be set forth before Thee as incense", *as incense seasoned with salt.*

JUNE 19

Isa. 64. 4 : R.V. *God . . . Which worketh for him that waiteth for Him.*

marginaliaWay

We have often taken this to mean that our God so guides and controls our outward affairs that confusion ends in peace; and this is true, but taken with Phil. 2. 13, we find an even deeper comfort. We want to be sincere. We do earnestly desire to mix salt in our incense at all times, but we fear lest we should fail. "You have not to do it in your unaided strength : it is God Who is all the while supplying the impulse, giving you the power to resolve, the strength to perform, the execution of His good pleasure."

JUNE 20

Distractions (1)

Often, when we are most in earnest to pray, we are tormented by wandering thoughts and distractions of all sorts. I have been reading some old books lately and find that exactly the same thing distressed others. "The noise of a fly", as one says, is enough to distract him. Do not fuss, do not worry, do not spend time wondering why that thought came just then or that other interruption was allowed (for that is playing into the enemy's hands); but as soon as you are conscious that you have been drawn away, peacefully come back again. "Return unto thy rest, O my soul."

Psa. 116. 7

JUNE 21

Distractions (2)

Faber describes these uncomfortable things as "unmannerly distractions [which] come and force my thoughts from Thee."

There will be times when we forget ourselves and everyone else and everything else, and are caught up, absorbed; there is no word for what this is. But it will not be so every day. There must be something salutary in the pressing through which prayer generally means. "When Thou saidst, Seek ye My face; my heart said unto Thee, Thy face, Lord, will I seek." There is a seeking; there is no seeing without that seeking. So the best way is to refuse to be entangled and worried and fussed, and as simply as a child would turn to one whom it loves, so turn to Him Whom our soul loveth and, distractions or no distractions, say to Him, "Thy face, Lord, will I seek."

Psa. 27. 8

JUNE 22

Unexpected answers (1)

This is the fruit of my morning's reading. It is not new, but it came to me as new.

God counts on us to accept whatever answer to our prayers He gives us, whether or not it be the answer that we wished and

Rom. 15. 30-32 expected. When Paul wrote to the Christians of Rome, he asked for the kind of prayer that is like wrestling with a strong (though unseen) enemy. He asked for prayer for three things, that his service (the offering of alms) might be acceptable to the Jewish Christians; that he might be delivered from the Jews who did not believe; that he might come to them—the Christians of Rome—with joy. The answer to the second of these three prayers was two years in a prison in Caesarea; the answer to the third was two years' imprisonment in Rome. In both cases his was the kind of imprisonment which required the prisoner's right hand to be chained to a soldier's left.

JUNE 23

Unexpected answers (2)

Not many of us love to be under a roof between walls, without being able to go out into the open air. Think what it must have meant to Paul to be not only indoors but never once alone. Think of being chained to a Roman soldier at all hours Rom. 15. 32 of the day and night. "That I may come unto you with joy by the will of God, and may with you be refreshed." There was not much natural joy and refreshment in coming as a chained prisoner.

Nothing was explained. Paul and the men and women of Rome were trusted to accept the unexplained and, like John the Baptist, not to be offended in their Lord.

Do you not think that a great deal of what we call faith is not worth the name? It is too flimsy to be called by so strong a word. Faith is the steel of the soul.

JUNE 24

Psa. 5. 3 : *O Lord; in the morning will I direct my prayer unto Thee, and will look up.*

Hab. 2. 1 "And will look up", will keep watch, like Habakkuk on his watch-tower. Have you ever found that your Father has answered a forgotten prayer? I have, and I always feel ashamed; it is so rude to forget. A "Prayer-and-Answer Notebook" helps one to remember. It is evidence, which even the devil cannot dispute, of traffic with Heaven. It kindles love;

"I love the Lord, because He hath heard". How often we have
had cause to say that. My first note-book turned up among
some old papers lately. To read the notes was like finding
sprays of verbena between the leaves of a book; you know how
astonishingly fragrant they can be. There was one little sentence
that belonged to a rainy Sunday morning when I was, I
suppose, about ten, so that leaf was about sixty years old, but
it might have been only just picked, for as I read the words I
remembered every detail of that prayer and that answer.

If any of you keep such a book do not forget that the answer
to many prayers is, "Wait", or sometimes, "No, not that, but
something else, which, when you see Me, you will know was a
far better thing."

JUNE 25

1 John 5. 14, 15 : *And this is the confidence that we have in
Him, that, if we ask anything according to His
will, He heareth us: And if we know that He
hear us, whatsoever we ask, we know that we
have the petitions that we desired of Him.*

Love gave us these words and only love can understand
them. One who loves his Father knows by a kind of Heavenly
instinct what he may ask for, and what he may not ask for. Or
if he be in any doubt, he ceases to ask anything and rests his
heart on his Lord's own prayer, "Thy will be done". So it is
that he has this confidence, and knows that he has the petitions
that he has desired of Him.

The words are not for casual use, or for any except those
who earnestly want to be His true lovers, to whom the lightest
wish of their Lord is a command. The least of us may be a
lover.

JUNE 26

1 John 5. 14, 15 : *This is the confidence . . . we know that we
have the petitions that we desired of Him.*

Prayer is as various as life. There is a prayer that is swift,
brief—a look, a thought; there is the long-drawn prayer of
long tension; the prayer whose instant first answer is peace;

the prayer that is just the pouring out of the heart—"Lord, all my desire is before Thee". And as to that desire, love does not need to explain itself to Love.

But though this be so, I have been thinking to-day of the kind of prayer that sooner or later we must learn to pray for one another. We must learn to pray far more for spiritual victory than for protection from battle-wounds, relief from their havoc, rest from their pain. We must reach the place where we bend all our prayers that way, or (for I do want to be honest) our chief prayers. Love cannot be without longing to shield and to relieve, and love is of God, so we may be at rest about this inseparable instinct and quality of love, for Love understands.

Looking back, I know that I have often put the lesser first in my prayers for my beloveds. I see now that we cannot enter into the fulness of the confidence of 1 John 5. 14, 15 and say without any shade of mental reservation, "We *know* that we have", unless our prayer is for God's greatest gift—spiritual triumph. This triumph is not deliverance from, but victory in, trial, and that not intermittent but perpetual.

JUNE 27

When we pray for something which we want very much, it is good to remember that our Father delights to give us joy and so there is no need to press Him as if He were unwilling. To do that always seems to me to be unkind. It is as if we had not a very loving Father.

Yet He has told us to ask for what our hearts desire and so it is right to ask, and to ask earnestly, only with this "if" in the depths of our hearts, "If it be Thy blessed will, if it be for Thy glory."

JUNE 28

Dan. 6. 10: *He went into his house; and his windows being open in his chamber toward Jerusalem, he kneeled upon his knees . . . and prayed.*

Daniel did not have to open his windows when he wanted to commune with his Lord. Apparently they were open, as our Indian windows are, all the time. Is it not a perfect picture of how we are meant to live? We do not have to spend even one minute in opening our windows, if our custom is to keep them open. To be earthly-minded, moved by self-love, self-pity, self-will—that trend of feeling which leads to self-occupation—is to close the shutters.

Are my windows open toward Jerusalem? Is my whole being, with all its various "windows", always open? Sometimes winds blow from one side or another and a window is blown shut. If that happens, do I know it at once?

Lord Jesus, let me know it at once. Do not let me go on with any windows shut or half-open. Lord, help me to keep my windows open continually toward Jerusalem.

JUNE 29

Dan. 6. 10: *His windows being open in his chamber toward Jerusalem.*

Daniel had only to kneel down upon his knees beside one of those windows, and at once he had access to the Father. Daniel's windows almost certainly were very small, set in a thick wall. We often feel that the windows of our chamber are very small—we see so little, know so little of our Heavenly Jerusalem—but a bird can fly through a very small window out into the wide blue air, and if our windows be open toward Jerusalem, we shall in heart and mind thither ascend.

JUNE 30

Saviour, in Whom we have access with confidence,
Lead us in prayer to-day;
Here at Thy feet we lay
All our desires; do Thou
Direct us now.

O loving Comforter, help our infirmities,
That which we know not teach;
Fashion our mortal speech
That we may know to pray
The Heavenly way.

JULY 1

Exod. 17. 16 : mar. *Because the hand of Amalek is against the throne of the Lord.*

Rev. 5. 6 : *In the midst of the throne . . . a Lamb as it had been slain.*

Psa. 17. 13 : *Arise, O Lord, disappoint him, cast him down.*

Have you noticed how the hand against the throne, and the Lamb as though it had been slain in the midst of the throne, are two great pictures of the Unseen which are closely linked together? It is by virtue of Calvary that we use the words of Psalm 17. 13, "Arise, O Lord, disappoint him [the Amalek of our day], cast him down".

Jehovah Nissi, disappoint
Thine ancient enemy.
Because Thy throne he hath defied,
By virtue of the Crucified
We claim the victory.

The Terrible would hold his prey,
O Lamb of God, command
The shining legions of the light
To put this Amalek to flight,
The Cause is in Thy hand.

Our hands be steady, then, until
The setting of the sun,
When sudden, through the cloudy skies,
The dawn shall break, the song shall rise,
The song of warfare won.

94

JULY 2

Exod. 13. 21 : *The Lord went before them . . . in cloud and in fire.*

So cloud and fire are bound up with thoughts of guidance. Each day for each Israelite began with the sight of the impenetrable Cloud. What was the day to bring of journeying or of waiting? He did not know. He saw the Cloud, that was all. So do our days begin. We may have a time-table, even so, we face the Unknown. We know not what a day may bring forth, but if we are following our Leader we know that we shall be led. The symbol of that leading is a Cloud, through which we cannot see.

> Great Leader, guide me by cloud or fire,
> Let me be loyal to Thy heart's desire.
> And lest I falter if the way be long,
> O let Thy joy be strength to me and song.

JULY 3

Exod. 24. 12 : *Come up to Me . . . and be there.*

When Moses went up, a cloud enfolded him. In that cool darkness he heard words which afterwards he spoke to the people in the heat and glaring light of the plain. So, day by day, as we look forward into the hours which seem to rush upon us, we see not clearness but a cloud. Then a Voice that we know calls softly, Come up to Me, and be here; the Cloud of the Unknown becomes for us then the very over-shadowing of the wings of the Lord; we sit down under His shadow with great delight, and His fruit is sweet to our taste. And this fruit, tasted first in the dark alone with Him, will be ours for others. "What I tell you in darkness", He says to us still, "that speak ye in light." *Song 2. 3*

Matt. 10. 27

JULY 4

Cloud and Fire

We cannot think of that pure element, fire, without thinking of the searching and the purification that must be if we are to hear and to understand the Voice of our God. Westcott quotes a Jewish legend about the Voice at Sinai; it sounded from everywhere; the people turned to the north—it came from the east; to the east—it came from the west. They lifted their eyes to the heavens—it came from the depths of the earth. Each one in Israel heard it according to his capacity. "The Voice was to each one as each one had power to receive it" (as in John 12. 28, 29).

A great sentence from the Apocrypha, "Their eyes saw the majesty of His glory and their ears heard the glory of His Voice," makes one feel how deeply those among them, who understood the holy mystery of that revelation, must have felt the need of a cleansing as by fire. Thank God then for the symbol of fire, for the reality of that which it symbolizes, for the promise that holds good for each of us, as we seek to hear His Voice and to follow the Pattern. "He shall sit [in His infinite patience, it is not the work of a moment] as a refiner and purifier of silver :" "I will turn My hand upon thee, and purely purge away thy dross, and take away all thy tin".

Mal. 3. 3

Isa. 1. 25

JULY 5

Exod. 25. 22 : *There I will meet with thee, and I will commune with thee from above the mercy-seat.*

In reading Exodus 25 I suddenly saw this, not a new thing, but you can imagine how it shone out : That which comes nearest and dearest of all—unhindered communion with our God—is based on His revealed will, accepted and obeyed. "The testimony that I shall give thee", He told Moses, was to be put in the Ark above which was to be the Mercy-seat. "And *there* I will meet with thee and will commune with thee."

Psa 143. 10

It is the old prayer again : "Teach me to do Thy will". I want to learn more and more what the small word "do" means as carried out in life. It is so much easier to pray about doing, and to talk to others about it, and to sing about it, than it is simply and honestly to do that very thing. But the prayer is not, Teach me to pray about it, talk about it, sing about it—though prayer and talk and song have their place—it is "Teach me *to do* Thy will". Then comes that beautiful blessed "*There* I will meet with thee and will commune with thee".

JULY 6

Exod. 27. 20 : *Pure olive oil beaten for the light, to cause the lamp to burn always.*

If the oil is to feed a lamp so that it burns continually, it must be pure. In how many ways the question is brought home to us! Are we willing for whatever is required for purification? Have we any mental reserve?

"Try me, O God, and seek the ground of my heart: prove me, and examine my thoughts." Psa. 139. 23
P.B.V.

JULY 7

Exod. 29. 43, 45 : *There I will meet with the children of Israel, and the tabernacle shall be sanctified by My glory . . . And I will dwell among the children of Israel, and will be their God.*

For many days the beautiful words translated from the old German of Ter Steegen have been in my heart:

> Am I not enough, Mine own? enough,
>   Mine own, for thee?

*   *   *   *   *   *

> All shalt thou find at last,
>   Only in Me.
> Am I not enough, Mine own? I, for ever
>   and alone, *I*, needing thee?

The ritual of the tabernacle, like the symbolism of its structure and furniture, led on to this: "And I will dwell among the children of Israel". "They shall call His Name Emmanuel, which being interpreted is, God with us." Is it not humbling and wonderful that such a God should wish to dwell with us, and so wish that He gave His very Dearest to make it possible? And He, that Well-beloved One, "died for desire of us". This thought is too great for us: "It is high, I cannot attain unto it." And yet, thank God, it is true. What does it mean to me to-day? Exod. 29. 45
Matt. 1. 23

Psa. 139. 6

JULY 8

Phil. 2. 13, 14 : (Rotherham) *It is God Who energizeth within you, both the desiring and the energizing, in behalf of His good pleasure. All things be doing, apart from murmurings and disputings.*

Have you ever connected these two verses? I do not think I ever did till to-day when I read from the one straight into the other.

The Bible is full of such looks into the mind of the Spirit; what we call great, and what we call small, are not divided into separate compartments. They run into one another. They are really one.

So to come down to your life and mine, this means we must not ask for easy things for each other. We must rather pray that we shall be so gloriously energized by the mighty power of God, that we shall do all things that come to be done, without a single inward grumble, making them our pleasure because they are His good pleasure.

JULY 9

We often think of life under the form of picture-words. Life is a fight, a wrestle, a journey, a race, a climb, and so on. This morning I was thinking of it as a voyage with no promise of calm seas. Then I came upon this in Psa. 89. 9 : "When the waves . . . arise, Thou stillest them."

Psa. 66. 20

So the call is always to confidence. "Blessed be God, Which hath not turned away my prayer, nor His mercy from

Psa. 89. 1

Psa. 9. 1

me." "I will sing of the mercies of the Lord for ever". "I will praise Thee, O Lord, with my whole heart". We are as nothing before the waves of the sea, whether they be big or

see Psa. 89. 19

little, but Thou hast "laid help upon One that is mighty". No waves that ever were or shall be can overwhelm us, if only we trust these words, "When the waves . . . arise, Thou stillest them."

JULY 10

1 Chron. 14. 15 : *God is gone forth before thee.*

"God, Who . . . in divers manners spake", speaks so still. This morning He spoke to me through two old Tamil proverbs. "Only by crossing the river can one reach the other shore", "What are hills and valleys to the horse of the King?" The LXX calls the valley of 1 Chron. 14. 13 the Giants' Valley. The word fits my inward need, for a letter full of power to disturb dropped into my Quiet like a stone flung into a pool, and much seemed to press round me of things to be done.

The Giants' Valley—but into that Valley the Lord went first. "God is gone . . . before thee". *Hills and valleys,* every sort of roughness, what are they to the power of the King? Then let us cross our rivers, and fear not our valleys, though they be Giants' Valleys. For the Lord is gone before. Always and everywhere He goeth before.

Heb. 1. 1

JULY 11

Rom. 8. 18 : *Not worthy to be compared.*

Settle this in your minds so that you will not have to settle it again; there is no promise of ease for any soldier on any field. Search the New Testament; you will not find one such promise. It is made quite clear that things are *not* going to be made easy. So to be surprised and troubled when they are difficult is foolish and unreasonable too. Why is there so much inward stress, sometimes sharp trial, or what the New Testament calls Tribulation? We are not told; but we are told that there will be this sort of thing, and that it is "not worthy to be compared with the glory"—*not worthy to be compared.*

JULY 12

Psa. 86. 17 : *A token for good.*

Look out for tokens for good, you who are fighting the good fight. The fight is good—no doubtful weapons are we ever called upon to use, thank God. Tokens for good are among the things we may ask and receive, as we fight on and do not allow ourselves to be dismayed or discouraged by the power of the great adversary.

Look out for them and you shall find them. Some will be little private tokens, something just between you and your Lord. Some will be things that you can share with others for their cheer. The great thing is not to miss them in the press of life, for often, very often, by these tokens for good our Lord helps us and comforts us. "Shew me a token for good; . . . because Thou, Lord, hast holpen me, and comforted me."

JULY 13

Dr F. B. Meyer once told me that when he was young he was very irritable, and an old man told him that he had found relief from this very thing by looking up the moment he felt it coming, and saying, "Thy sweetness, Lord." By telling this, that old man greatly helped Dr Meyer, and he told it to tens of thousands. I pass it on to you because I have found it a certain and a quick way of escape. Take the opposite of your temptation and look up inwardly, naming that opposite; Untruth—Thy truth, Lord; Unkindness—Thy kindness, Lord; Impatience—Thy patience, Lord; Selfishness—Thy unselfishness, Lord; Roughness—Thy gentleness, Lord; Discourtesy—Thy courtesy, Lord; Resentment, inward heat, fuss—Thy sweetness, Lord, Thy calmness, Thy peacefulness.

I think that no one who tries this very simple plan will ever give it up. (It takes it for granted, of course, that all is yielded—the "I" dethroned.) Will all to whom it is new try it for a day, a week, a month, and test it?

JULY 14

Psa. 71. 16
P.B.V.

Psa. 68. 28
P.B.V.
The Psalm for the 14th day of the month gives us this : *I will go forth in the strength of the Lord God* : the perfect word coming after "Thy God hath sent forth strength for thee". Often the Psalms most marvellously follow one another in a great procession, as if our God had guided those who strung them together like pearls on a string—as I am sure He did.

He has sent forth strength for our day's life, so we will go forth into our day in the strength of the Lord.

If at any time in the day we find ourselves in need, we may pray, "Be Thou my Strong-hold, whereunto I may alway resort"; and if ·we find ourselves missing something that we naturally desire—"Thou, O Lord God, art the thing that I long for" brings us back to our Rest. Psa. 71. 2
P.B.V.

v. 4. P.B.V.

JULY 15

Luke 10. 19 : *I give unto you power to tread on serpents and scorpions, and over all the power of the enemy: and nothing shall by any means hurt you.*

Our Lord Jesus said this to the seventy : and yet we know that all down the ages His servants have been hurt in a thousand ways. So the words must mean, and we know they do mean, something that goes far deeper than bodily hurt, deeper even than disappointment—that hardest hurt the mind can be asked to bear.

It must mean that our *spirits* shall tread on serpents and scorpions, and have power over all the enemy. Nothing shall be able to sting our spirit, poison it, or paralyse it. It is one of the magnificent promises of the Bible. We cannot take it too literally. There is no need to be overcome, whatever happens. "O my soul, thou hast trodden down strength." Judges 5. 21

JULY 16

Sometimes we do not feel in the least like treading down scorpions and serpents and all the power of the enemy. Perhaps we are allowed to feel our nothingness, so that we may in the depths of our heart understand those other words "Without Me ye can do nothing." I think there was something of this in our Lord Jesus' mind, when He told the story of one who had nothing to set before his friend—not a crumb—and it was midnight. When we do not feel victorious and have nothing to give to others, it is in truth "midnight" in our soul, "the dark night of the soul", old writers called it. Luke 10. 19

John 15. 5

Luke 11. 5-8

But we have a God to Whom we can go at any minute, the weakest minute, the darkest minute, "at midnight". "Be Thou my strong habitation, whereunto I may continually resort : Psa. 71. 3

Luke 11. 8

Thou hast given commandment to save me; for Thou art my Rock and my Fortress." And if it be victory over the power of the enemy in our own hearts that we need, He will give us not just crumbs, but loaves—"He will rise and give him as many as he needeth."

JULY 17

Num. 13. 16

One day in a talk about Joshua I was reminded of his change of name from Oshea (Salvation) to Joshua (Jehovah is my Salvation). As I read the book of Joshua and thought of his military operations, that change of name was constantly in my mind. What a difference it would make in the conduct of every campaign if only all who call themselves Christians had truly gone through that change of name which means, of course, a change of character.

The Lord lead further and further those who do in earnest want to live the Joshua life. It means a daily dying to self and what self wants; a daily turning to our Master with a "Yes, Lord" to everything, even to what is most against the grain. May He quicken those who have not yet begun to live this life to see what they are missing, before it is too late.

JULY 18

Psa. 90. 14 : *O satisfy us early with Thy mercy; that we may rejoice and be glad all our days.*

What a contrast this is to the "labour and sorrow" referred to in verse 10. Surely the Bible is a book of glorious paradoxes.

As I thought of this, I remembered times when toil for souls seemed "labour and sorrow" in vain, and I know that among you there are sure to be some who, from time to time, are tempted to feel like that. Our Lord must have been tempted in the same way about Judas, for we know that He "was in all points tempted like as we are". But He lived in the power of verse 14. He was not the "Man of Sorrows" only, He was anointed with the oil of gladness above His fellows.

Heb. 4. 15

Psa. 45. 7

There is a tremendously uplifting power in joy. Perhaps that is why there is so much about it in the Bible. It may be that if only we live in the power of Psalm 90. 14 "all our days", we shall find at the end that our Lord used the joy that He gave us, to help not only those nearby, but some whom we never met in the flesh, though how that can be I do not know.

So, satisfied with His mercy, let us rejoice and be glad all our days—all these days, this day.

JULY 19

Psa. 37. 8 : P.B.V. *Let go displeasure.*

Sometimes something happens which recalls great pain. You are not able to find pleasure in that thing. You are oppressed by it and saddened. Suddenly the word comes, "Let go displeasure".

Displeasure is not always wrath; it is not unkindness, or the fretting which the Psalm says so truly, "tendeth only to evil-doing." It is just something that is not pleasure but pain, and so can depress the heart. R.V.

Let it go. Do not hold on to it. Let it slip out of mind. Turn to something that does give pleasure and fasten your thoughts on that. "Hold thee still in the Lord, and abide patiently upon Him." "Commit thy way" (and the way of those thou lovest) unto Him, and thou shalt "be refreshed in the multitude of peace." v. 7 P.B.V.
v. 5 P.B.V.
v. 11 P.B.V.

Prove this word if ever you are tempted in this way. You will find that by an act of will, by His grace, you can "let go displeasure" and be most tenderly released and refreshed.

JULY 20

Words

More than half the troubles that come to us come because of words. There is a question that has often helped me : "Wherefore hearest thou men's words?" 1 Sam. 24. 9

I suggest that next time you are afflicted by words you should let that quiet question do its work in your heart. No one yet did anything worth doing without finding, sooner or later, that words buzzed about him (or her) in a most distressing way.

Psa. 57. 7

May the Lord help us to go on lovingly, peacefully, steadfastly. "My heart is fixed, O God, my heart is fixed : I will sing and give praise." One look up into the face of our Lord, and the thought of any hurting word melts like a little cloud in the blue of the sky above us. And if it be so now, what will it be when we see Him, Whom we have not yet seen, face to face?

Mark 8. 23 : *He took the blind man by the hand, and led him out of the town.*

Will this Note find someone puzzled about anything, in the dark, as we say, about what they should do?

This morning I was reading through the Gospel of Mark, noticing each place where our Lord Jesus suffered anything, or spoke of suffering, and as I read, words that have nothing to do with that special subject caught my eye : "He took the blind man by the hand, and led him out of the town".

There is a town of the noise of words, the noise of other people's words, and of our own words, too, as we talk to ourselves and listen to the confusion of our thoughts and desires as they talk within us. There is only One Who can take the blind by the hand, and lead him out of the town. The hand that led that man was soon to be pierced. Soon after this incident we come to the words, "The Son of Man must suffer" —it is a suffering Christ Who leads us out of the town and along the road that leads to clearness of vision, and then to Calvary. But the road does not stop there. It goes over the hill to the Other Side.

JULY 22

Heb. 12. 2

Calvary is never the end of the road for the blind man whom the Lord leads by the hand out of the town, and to whom He gives vision. "Who for the joy that was set before Him endured the Cross" is a great word for fainting souls.

As I read the New Testament over and over, I am more and more impressed by the way suffering was taken for granted as something appointed; but always there is the thought of joy not

far off. In our Lord's private talks with His disciples, there is
continually and clearly that "Must" of suffering, and the joy to
follow. We often act as if the place that is called Calvary had
been taken out of the landscape of life, or were an accident
there. It is not so; but just out of sight is the joy that is set
before us, and there is the power which can enable us to treat
the invisible as visible, the promised as present.

JULY 23

Matt. 20. 23 : *Ye shall indeed drink of My cup, and be baptized with the baptism that I am baptized with.*

These words have been the food on which I have fed during
the last three days. Some of the Lord's followers have the
greatest of all surprises of joy. They are like James, who with
one stroke of the sword was with his Lord. Others, like John,
have set before them the long road of life. To these two for
whom such contrasting experiences were appointed, this word
was spoken. Both drank of the cup; both were baptized with
the baptism; but there is, I think, no comparison between the
two tests of faith appointed. The beloved disciple was, I
suppose, the most sensitive of all to pain as well as to joy, and
yet the test to which he was called was incomparably the
harder.

But think of the wonder of it—if by a quick sharp release one
drank of the cup, the other equally drank of it as he lived to
serve. As we look back upon this "little while", it will indeed
seem only a little while, and all that will matter then will be
that we drank of the cup, were baptized with the baptism.

JULY 24

John 3. 14 : (an ancient Version) *The Son of Man is ready to
be lifted up.*

"The Son of Man is ready", ready then, ready always, never
unprepared for whatever the next step was to be.

This was a word to me one day lately, and soon after reading
it I had to ask someone to do a difficult thing. It was such a joy
to find readiness, readiness without human preparation. I

realized then the joy that our Lord must have been to His Father, and the joy that, in our measure, we too may be to Him.

Often I think we sing and pray a little beyond what we are really prepared to be and do, and sometimes God comes to us and says, Now live what you sang to Me yesterday, or, Live what you have taught others, or, Are you willing to *do* this, not just to pray to Me about it?

2 Sam. 15. 15 And the King's servants said unto the King, Behold, Thy servants are ready to do whatsoever our Lord the King shall appoint.

JULY 25

John 2. 5 : *Whatsoever He saith unto you, do it.*

Yesterday when I read these words, I thought how good it would be if all of us heard and obeyed them.

v. 4 They were spoken just after our Lord Jesus had said, Let Me follow out My own course (this is what Westcott says is the meaning of the words He used to Mary)—if you love Me, trust Me.

Mary understood her Son and Lord. So she said very simply to the servants, Whatsoever He tells you to do, do it.

If there be love in our hearts, there will be confidence, and we shall be ready to say to ourselves just what Mary said to the servants (without any ifs or buts), "Whatsoever He saith unto you, do it."

JULY 26

Isa. 55. 3 : *Come unto Me: hear, and your soul shall live.*

We may read, we may listen, we may even feel, without once truly hearing in this sense. The Lord open our ears that we may hear, and live the life that is life indeed; the life St Paul lived from the hour when for the first time he truly heard; the life Acts 26. 19 that is "not disobedient to the Heavenly vision", but presses on 1 Sam. 3. 9 from day to day, walking in newness of life. "Speak, Lord; for Thy servant heareth." "Hear, and your soul shall live."

JULY 27

John 3. 21 : *He that doeth truth cometh to the light, that his deeds may be made manifest, that they are wrought in God.*

Each new day will give us a chance to do truth, and to come to the light from which nothing is hid. If there be anything about which it cannot be said that it was wrought in God (that is, in the power of His Spirit; for His glory, not for our own), then if we love Him we shall want this to be made manifest, so that we may have done with it, and all may be pure in His sight. "The world passeth away, and the lust thereof : but he that doeth the will of God abideth for ever." 1 John 2. 17

JULY 28

Psa. 132. 11 : P.B.V. *The Lord hath made a faithful oath unto David: and He shall not shrink from it.*

As I read the Psalms for the day these words took on a new meaning. Other translations have "He will not turn from it". He will not recall His word. He will not annul it. When we remember Calvary, and how the fulfilment of His promise meant nothing less than the crucifixion of the Son of His love, then (speaking humanly) we can understand why the Father might have shrunk from so tremendous a sacrifice; but He did not.

In this Psalm, which is the only Psalm where the Ark is mentioned (the type of His perpetual Presence with us), He says He will not shrink from carrying out that which alone makes that holy Presence possible. The use of the word made me understand His tenderness in a new way. He knows that the temptation to us is to shrink from anything which is very difficult to face; but He, Who did not shrink, can strengthen *us* not to shrink.

Place on the Lord reliance,
My soul, with courage wait,
His truth be thine affiance
When faint and desolate

J. Montgomery.

JULY 29

Exod. 15. 25 : *The Lord shewed him a tree.*

This is a word which was spoken to me. "The Lord showed him a tree, which when he had cast into the waters, the waters were made sweet".

We all know what the Tree means. Nothing less than the powers of Calvary can turn our bitter waters into sweet waters.

vv. 23-25

> O Marah pool, set in the desert sands,
>   How can we drink, how can we drink of thee?
>   But Moses cried, and he was shown a tree.
> Did ever heart in vain Thy grace entreat?
> Touch of the tree made bitter waters sweet.
>
> So, blessed Lord, in all our Marah days,
>   Show us the Tree; one thought of Calvary's Cross
>   Makes bitter sweet, discovers gain in loss.
> Let not your heart be troubled, Thou didst say
> Long, long ago. It is Thy word today.

JULY 30

"The pattern of Christ, as set before us in the New Testament, is in every case a pattern of humiliation, suffering, sacrifice." *"In every case"*. This made me search for confirmation or otherwise of so strong a statement, though I knew that the writer (Westcott) would not have made it unless he had been sure that it was true. Perhaps the question comes, We have common work to do (gardening, sewing, cooking, and so on), what have these three great words, Humiliation, Suffering, Sacrifice, to do with us?

Humiliation : Do we like to be praised? Do we find it difficult if mistakes are shown? Which matters most to us—that the work should be well done or that people should know that we did that work? Is our "I" in the dust?

Suffering : When we stand for truth are we ever misunderstood? Then what do we do?

Sacrifice : What comes first in our choice—our Lord's wish or our own?

If we answer these questions honestly I think we shall understand how we can begin to learn to follow the pattern set by Christ our Lord. He must have begun to follow that pattern when, to the eyes of the village, He was just a boy in a carpenter's shop.

JULY 31

Isa. 63. 7 : *I will mention the lovingkindnesses of the Lord, and the praises of the Lord, according to all that the Lord hath bestowed on us, and the great goodness toward the house of Israel, which He hath bestowed on them according to His mercies, and according to the multitude of His lovingkindnesses.*

These words came to me last night as for the first time. I read them over and over again, and each time they seemed more beautiful and satisfying. They are lovely words for the last day of another month.

Everything, even the hard things, are wrapped up in the lovingkindnesses of the Lord, and His lovingkindnesses "have been ever of old."   Psa. 25. 6

AUGUST 1

Love through me, Love of God,
　There is no love in me;
O Fire of love, light Thou the love
　That burns perpetually.

Flow through me, Peace of God,
　Calm river flow until
No wind can blow, no current stir
　A ripple of self-will.

Shine through me, Joy of God,
　Make me like Thy clear air
That Thou dost pour Thy colours through,
　As though it were not there.

O blessed Love of God,
　That all may taste and see
How good Thou art, once more I pray,
　Love through me, even me.

AUGUST 2

*Oh, let the glow of Thy great love
Through my whole being shine.*
　　　　　　　　　J. C. Lavater.

1 Pet. 4. 8 : *Above all things have fervent charity among
　　　　　yourselves.*

1 Pet. 1. 22 : *Love one another with a pure heart fervently.*

Acts 18. 25　Apollos was "fervent in the spirit"—the word means *to boil,*
Rom. 12. 11　*be hot* or fervid as in Paul's "Be ... fervent in spirit". (It was
Titus 3. 13　this Apollos, he of the fervent heart, whom Paul wanted to
have with him in prison.)

110

There are a great many Orders in the world. I should like to think that we all belonged to *The Order of the Fervent Heart.* If we are anywhere but in the Love of God, we drift apart. If any have been cooling, drifting, if any are not warm in love towards one another, will they not find time for drawing near once more, first to their Lord, then, as His love re-kindles them, to one another?

AUGUST 3

Sometimes people say how hard it is to be loving to those who do not seem to care at all about our Lord Jesus.

We cannot think without sorrow and pity of those who have night in their hearts, just as we cannot think of one who is in the dark night of blindness, without longing that he could see. But this is not enough to hold us in love. The only thing that will do that is the very love of God. "God commendeth His Rom. 5. 8 R.V. own love toward us, in that, while we were yet sinners, Christ died for us." It is this love, the love that loves the unlovable, that we must have. Nothing less will do. He is willing to give it. Next time we are tempted to a feeling of "unlove" let us try the way of which we thought some weeks ago, and looking up, say quickly, Thy love, Lord.

May He Who is our Beloved, give it to us who are His lovers to be even as the sunflowers that turn to the sun, and looking on Him to be like Him.

AUGUST 4

1 John 4. 16 : *And we have known and believed the love that God hath to us. God is love; and he that dwelleth in love dwelleth in God, and God in him.*

What I specially want to bring you is this : young children and all who do not know our Lord have only one way of knowing how loving He is. They look at us. If there be any flaw in our love, if we fail them at any point, we make it just so much the harder for them to see, to know, to apprehend, His love. Do not let us fail our children. "Love through me, Love of God".

AUGUST 5

There is a wonderful happiness in being loved, we all know it; but the further we go on, the more we know that what matters most is not to be loved, but to love. Yet we cannot help a child unless we have its love (nor an older soul, either, nor indeed anyone). So, I think that God, knowing this, gives to those who have to do with souls, mother-love, father-love, the kind of love that draws out the (perhaps hidden) powers of love in that soul, even as sunshine after rain draws the flowers from the bulb underground.

Should any of us feel as though the love which we must have, if we are to help anyone, is beginning to run dry (dried up, perhaps over some very difficult soul) think of the Fountain. It never runs dry. "Love through me, Love of God".

AUGUST 6

One night in a dream someone seemed to ask me, If you were writing your last note to your children what would it be about? And I said, It would begin with these words, *"Beloved, let us love"*. And the voice said, Write it now; so I began to write that note, but cannot remember a word of what I wrote except these four words, "Beloved, let us love".

This is not, I think, anywhere near my last note, but even so, I am writing these words for you to-day. Are there any of you out of love? Have any a feeling of unlove about any? Has anyone said anything about another which would hinder prayer, if you and that one were alone together? Is there any least thought of unlove anywhere? O Love of God, search us and see. O Love, Thou art Light, search us and see. Cleanse us, prepare us to draw near to Thee, alone or together, unhindered by the least unlove. "Beloved, let us love".

AUGUST 7

1 John 4. 7 : *Beloved, let us love.*

As I prayed afresh for His love, I could only think of these words of the disciple who, perhaps more tenderly than any other, entered into the thought of his Lord. Again and again in one way or another he expressed this thought. May each one

1 John 4. 7

of us go further into this life of love than ever we have gone before.

We have so many prayer-songs about love that I do not like to add another, and yet this very short and simple one has come, and perhaps some of you may find that it says what you want to say:

"What wouldest thou that I should do for thee?"
My Lord, my Saviour, pour Thy love through me.

As mountain river when its streams run dry,
So, but for Thee, Fountain of Love, am I.

If there be hindrance, sweep it all away,
O Love Eternal, pour through me, I pray.

AUGUST 8

The Three Sieves
Is it true?   Is it kind?   Is it necessary?

All of us who have tried to remember these three sieves, and have used them, know what a help they are. We are sorry when we ever forget them, and we are very grateful when we are reminded of them in time to keep us from saying something untrue, unkind, or unnecessary.

Sometimes when I listen to hymn-singing I think of the words about the fig tree and the vine and the fountain. "Can the fig tree . . . bear olive berries? either a vine, figs? So can no fountain both yield salt water and fresh." Can the lips which have sung these beautiful loving words speak those other words? But they sometimes do.

Jas. 3. 12

Perhaps these three sieves will help to keep some words from being spoken that would grieve the Spirit of love and hurt someone whom our Lord loves.

Is it true? Is it kind? Is it necessary?

AUGUST 9

The three sieves are only useful for keeping wrong words from being spoken. They do not give us right words. Love can fill the cup so full of love, that nothing can come out but love. You remember the old illustration.[1] Love can quicken our powers of thinking and of imagining so that we shall know how others are feeling, even if they do not tell us; a kind of instinct will tell us—the instinct of love. Love will never let us hurt another unless we must, and then it will hurt us far more. We will not do it easily.

Sometimes there is a great deal to be done before God can come upon us in changing and renewing power. But if only we will ask Him to come now and sweep from us every particle of unlove; to cleanse us thoroughly in this matter, searching into the deep places of our hearts, where thoughts that only He and we know like to creep and hide; then the way will be clear for Him to do all that He longs to do for us.

AUGUST 10

Prov. 8. 30, 31 : *I was daily His delight, rejoicing always before Him; rejoicing in the habitable part of His earth; and My delights were with the sons of men.*

And yet some of the sons of men would crucify Him; and in a certain part of the habitable earth was the little hill which we know as Calvary.

I do not think any verse in the Old Testament shows the glorious conquering love of Christ more than this verse. He, knowing all, yet loves; and His love is not defeated by our sin and weakness. If only we give eternal love the right of way, that love will perfect all that concerneth us, for the Lord did not set love upon us because of any good He saw in us, but "because the Lord loved".

Deut. 7. 7, 8

I cannot tell you how often this has held my heart in hope, when there was nothing in all the world to give me any ground for hope. And the Revised Version makes the blessed words even more blessed, "Because the Lord *loveth* you".

---

[1] A cup brimful of sweet water cannot spill even one drop of bitter water however suddenly jolted.

AUGUST 11

One day last week a troubled heart told me of a thought which perhaps some of you have, How can I love many people? I can love some very much, but there is not room in my heart for many. I spoke to her of the bees and of how cell after cell is added to the comb and each is filled with sweet honey.

Each cell is so shaped that the greatest possible number can be fitted into the smallest possible space. God, Who taught the bees to do this, can do something as wonderful for us; He can add a new cell to our heart as each new person (child or grown-up) comes to be loved; and He can fill the cell full of the sweet honey of His love.

AUGUST 12

Rom. 10. 21 : (Rotherham) *All day long have I stretched forth My hands unto a people unyielding and contradicting.*

To-day this verse which has often helped me came in my reading. When I have been near the end of my patience with some unyielding child, or some "contradicting" disposition, these words have come to me. He Who gave us our work to do knows all about it, and has been through that sense of baffled love. He is with us now, and all the day long His hands are stretched forth. His love never faileth. Lord, evermore give us this love.

AUGUST 13

Col. 3. 13 : *Forbearing one another, and forgiving one another, if any man have a quarrel against any.*

There is a sentence in Bishop Moule's *Colossian Studies* which is on my heart to pass on to you; it is this : "Pardoning; hoping; loving; bearing with one another, and forgiving one another, if (the *if* puts, as it were, reluctantly, a case just supposable) anyone has a grievance against anyone; (for you are erring sinners still, and may give each other occasion for such victories of good over evil). Just as the Lord did forgive you, so do you too."

"Occasion for such victories" is a beautiful way of putting it. It has helped me, not once but countless times. In a family there may be ("for we are erring sinners still") these "occasions". If such come our way, let us use them for the loveliest of all lovely purposes—victories of love.

AUGUST 14

Love of my heart, my stream runs dry;
    O Fountain of the heavenly hills,
Love, blessed Love, to Thee I cry,
    Flood all my secret hidden rills.
Waters of love, O pour through me,
I must have Love: I must have Thee.

Lord, give me love, then I have all,
    For love casts out tormenting fear.
And love sounds forth a trumpet call
    To valiant hope; and sweet and clear
The birds of joy sing in my tree,
Love of my heart, when I have Thee.

AUGUST 15

For the tempted. (1)
Psa. 77. 3 : P.B.V. *When I am in heaviness, I will think upon God.*

Have you noticed how, when you are in heaviness, you are always tempted to think about yourself—your uselessness, your failures, your nothingness—yourself in one way or another? I have known this temptation and constantly found it tormenting others. To draw one's thoughts to oneself is a long-tried and most successful wile of the devil. Straight against this is the word we have in this Psalm, "When I am in heaviness, I will think upon God". I will turn my thoughts from myself to my Father Who loves me and does not stop loving me, though I am useless and a failure and less than nothing at all.

AUGUST 16

For the tempted. (2)

Another word in Psa. 77 that has helped me again and again is *v.* 10. "And I said, It is mine own infirmity : but I will remember the years of the right hand of the Most Highest." **P.B.V.**

A thousand questions crowd : "Will the Lord absent Himself for ever?" is only the first of a swarm of painful questions. We do not feel, we do not see, we cannot pray, it is as if His lovingkindness were shut up from us, "clean gone for ever". And all the time that love is holding us, clasping us, though we feel nothing of its tenderness and strength. **v. 7 P.B.V.**

v. 8

At such times the one and only way is the old way, "I will remember . . ." My God abideth faithful, so, feelings or no feelings, "I will trust and not be afraid". In this lies the way of release from the oppression of the enemy. "Who is so great a God as our God?" **Isa. 12. 2**

Psa. 77. 13

AUGUST 17

For the tempted. (3)

When we are tried by dryness, dullness of heart and despair, we are very likely to feel alone in that most unhappy state. Perhaps that is why our wonderful Father took care to have such writings as Psa. 77 preserved for us. There are many such passages in the Bible, but I think this Psalm and Psalm 88 show the most concentrated essence of spiritual distress we find anywhere. Yet it clearly shows the way out into the sunshine. Verse 11 (like *v.* 3 and *v.* 10 P.B.V.) shows the way: it calls memory to our aid: "I will remember the works of the Lord: and call to mind Thy wonders of old time."

It may seem quite impossible that we should rise and triumph, but "Thou art the God that doeth wonders". We do not understand this strange way; be it so. "Thy way is in the sea". Who can find footsteps in the sea? Even so, even there, "Thou leddest Thy people like sheep". **v. 14 P.B.V.**

v. 19

v. 20 P.B.V.

AUGUST 18

For the tempted. (4)

P.B.V. In the next Psalm (78) there is a beautiful reassuring word for all who are going through what an old writer called "the dark night of the soul".

v. 15 "In the daytime also He led them with a cloud : and all the night through with a light of fire." So there were nights as well as days appointed for His people of old. There were rocky v. 16 days, too, when everything seemed to go wrong. But "He clave the hard rocks in the wilderness", and, wonder of wonders, out of those very rocks "gave them drink thereof, as it had been out of the great depth".

The water He gives to us from these deep places is clear cool water, water we can give to others, with the certainty that if only they will drink they will find it living water, and their thirst will be quenched.

AUGUST 19

I have often longed to save those whom I love from the strain and stress of suffering, but I never could; and to-day I have read these words in Conybeare's translation of Rom. 5. 3-5 :

"We know that by suffering is wrought steadfastness, and steadfastness is the proof of soundness, and proof gives rise to hope; and our hope cannot shame us in the day of trial; because the love of God is shed forth in our hearts by the Holy Spirit, Who has been given unto us."

Suffering, steadfastness, soundness, hope, love—what great words these are, and how arresting is the order in which they are set. We may not change the order. Eternal Love set them in that order and Eternal Love will justify that order if only we go on in peace and are never offended in Him.

AUGUST 20

I have always noticed that when God has purposes of blessing for some soul, the devil of discouragement, who is one of Satan's most useful servants, is sure to come and whisper all sorts of sorrowful, depressing, miserable thoughts. He drops these thoughts about, sometimes in one heart and sometimes in another. If they take root and grow into feelings and words and deeds, he knows that a great deal has been done to hinder what our God intends to do.

Do not forget that discouragement is always from beneath; encouragement is always from above; God is the God of Encouragement.

AUGUST 21

Some of us need faith to meet very hard things, and love for very hard-to-love people, the love that will not be tired out of loving. Here is a little prayer-song for this:

> O Beloved of my soul,
>   This do I desire :
> Faith for the impossible,
>   Love that will not tire.
> Jesus, Saviour, Lover, give me
> Love for the unlovable,
>   Love that will not tire.
>
> O Beloved of my soul,
>   Yet again I come;
> Give me cords of love to draw
>   Many wanderers home.
> Jesus, Saviour, Lover, give me
> Love that knows nor strain nor flaw,
>   Love to lead them home.

AUGUST 22

Luke 4. 40 : *He laid His hands on every one of them, and healed them.*

This verse took life for me one day lately. I was reading in the Revised Version and looked up the Authorized, to see if I was reading something new, for it felt new. But no, I must have read it hundreds of times before.

"On every one of them". It comforted me to know that He does not look upon us as a mass, but as separate needy souls. I remembered the terrific attack that is always on the love that should hold us together, and I read over and over again John 15. 9-17. I know well that the devil hates and fears strong love. If he can weaken us there, all goes. For us, to weaken means to perish. I found rest in remembering the hands laid on every one of us, not one of us overlooked, and the hands laid upon us are wounded hands.

AUGUST 23

When we suffer, sometimes one of our first prayers is that others whom we love may not suffer in that way. This is just a faint reflection of His love, for He, Who was led into the wilderness to be tempted of the devil, taught us to pray, Lead us not into temptation. Yet often we are sorely tempted. Help comes by remembering that love is behind even that. "This is My beloved Son, in Whom I am well pleased. Then was Jesus led up of the Spirit into the wilderness". There is wonderful comfort in that *Then*.

And there is comfort waiting in words like "They thirsted not when He led them through the deserts." The Bible is full of such words. We each of us, probably, have our own special word. But if one comfort can be greater than another, when all are Divine, I would put this as the most precious: out of wilderness experience our wonderful Lord gives us something to use for the help of others. It was so with Him: "In that He Himself hath suffered being tempted, He is able to succour them that are tempted." Is it not worth while to go through anything if only in the end others may be helped?

Matt. 3. 17
Matt. 4. 1
Isa 48. 21
Heb. 2. 18

AUGUST 24

Deut. 2. 3: *Ye have compassed this mountain long enough: turn you northward.*

It would take too long to tell what this word has said to me. I will only say it spoke about a mountain of thought round which I have walked rather often. It is time to stop compassing that mountain.

After settling that matter, I remembered one who for two whole years has been walking round a certain Mountain of Desire. When the desired thing was not given at the expected time, there was great disappointment. Perhaps the Lord is saying to that one and to others who are constantly praying about something personally desired, Leave the matter to Me: you have prayed enough about it. You have compassed that mountain long enough.

I know another who always seems to be walking round a mountain of rubble. Self and the feelings of self, doubts and questions, grumblings, little piled-up ingratitudes—what are these but rubble? Is it not very dull to keep on compassing so dull a mountain? Hear the heartening word of the Lord, *ye have compassed this mountain long enough: turn you northward.* "Rise ye up, take your journey," (*v.* 24) "fight the good fight of faith," begin to possess your possessions.

1 Tim. 6. 12
Obad. 17

AUGUST 25

The story of Mary breaking her pot of ointment made me think of some among us who love their Saviour and yet have not broken theirs. Something is held back, and so there is no out-pouring of that love, no fragrance in the house. It is shut up, not given.

John 12. 3

The days are passing so quickly. Soon it will be too late to pour all we have on His feet. How sorry Mary would have been if she had missed her opportunity that evening—an opportunity that would never come again : "Me ye have not always." Soon He was among His foes. She could not have reached Him then.

v. 8

AUGUST 26

Psa. 27. 9 : LXX. *O God my Saviour, overlook me not.*

Have you ever felt overlooked? In old days to obey the God of Heaven often meant experiences like that of Jeremiah when he was let down into the dungeon where there was no water, but mire; and far oftener than not, there was no Ebed-melech. The prisoner was just overlooked. To how many hearts the temptation must have come to feel forsaken of God as well as

Jer. 38. 10

man. All down the ages there have been lives full of suffering, such tragedy of suffering that nothing but a miracle of love could have carried them through. To them the temptation to wonder if God cared must have been tremendous. Thinking of such lives we are ashamed that we are ever tempted to be down-hearted; but we have a Father Who understands the weakest and most foolish of His children. So, scattered through His Book, we have little simple prayers like this: "O God, my Saviour, overlook me not." "Do Thou for me, O God the Lord".

Psa. 109. 21

AUGUST 27

Rom. 8. 21: *Delivered from the bondage of corruption into the glorious liberty of the children of God.*
Rom. 8. 23: *Waiting for . . . the redemption of our body.*

"The bondage of corruption"—"The redemption of our body", and Young gives the meaning of redemption here as, *a loosing away*—a loosing away from the bondage. A loosing away "into the glorious liberty of the children of God"—that is what waits for us round the next corner of the road. No wonder Paul says that "the sufferings of this present time are not worthy to be compared with the glory which shall be revealed in us", and by suffering, do not let us forget he means the tremendous sufferings of those days, and of these days, too, in many places. So, where do our little trials of faith and patience and courage come in? They are small indeed. But even though they be small they can be real, and so I give you this glorious word which brought new life to me this morning. There is nothing eternal in our bonds, but the loosing is eternal. "By His own Blood He entered in once into the holy place, having obtained eternal redemption [eternal *loosing*] for us."

v. 18

Heb. 9. 12

AUGUST 28

Mark 9. 24, Aramaic: *I do believe: help my little belief.*

For some of us it is hard to accept the commands of which I wrote: "Think it not strange", "Count it all joy". Again and again we are tempted, for this kind of temptation is not the

kind that comes once and then disappears; it reappears when
we least expect it. Yet we do trust our God; we do believe that
if there had been· anything better than what is, that better thing
would have been chosen for us. We do believe that when we
look back at the end of the journey, we shall see how perfect
the way was—every mile of it. Why then are we tempted at all?

Perhaps in no other way could we be so cast upon our God,
or brought so low at His feet. If we never "suffered being
tempted", we could never know the depths of His understanding sympathy. We could never find the comfort that is in these
words. "I do believe; help my little belief."

Heb. 2. 18

AUGUST 29

Disheartened.

Sometimes we are inclined to think that it does not much
matter if we feel disheartened. We cannot help feeling so, we
say to ourselves, and perhaps we let ourselves slip into a disheartened frame of mind, without in the least realizing the
deadly danger that is near to the disheartened.

When the King of Babylon took Jerusalem (B.C. 539) and
carried certain of the people off to Babylon, he took those who
"fell away" to him, (*deserted*, the Revised Version says) and in
Rotherham the words are translated "the disheartened who
fell away unto him." If to be *disheartened* is the first step towards
falling away, deserting the flag, playing the traitor, we cannot
think of that state of mind as "not mattering much." Are we
yielding to the deadly influences that make us feel disheartened? Is there a cloud over our spirits that makes the
things we are doing seem not worth-while? That is the first
step down the slippery incline that leads to a base desertion and
a wretched captivity. But we need not slip one step further.
"When I said, My foot slippeth; Thy mercy, O Lord, held me
up."

Jer. 39. 9

Psa. 94. 18

AUGUST 30

Horns and Carpenters.

"I see such difficulties, I hardly know how to go on." Most
of us have said this, or felt it, at one time or another. We have

Zech. 1. 18-21

it here: "I lifted up mine eyes, and saw, and behold four horns." "I saw . . . four horns"—those powers that scatter and shatter and spoil, the cruel powers that blast good work, and discourage souls, "so that no man did lift up his head"—"I saw" them.

"And the Lord shewed me four carpenters"—those powers that put right what is wrong, that "fray" (frighten away, terrify) the evil powers—"the Lord shewed me" them.

We see the horns ourselves, but until the Lord opens our eyes we do not see the carpenters, and yet they are as truly present as the horns.

Matt. 28. 18, 20

"All power is given unto Me in Heaven and in earth, . . . and lo, I am with you alway"—"all the days and all the day

Mark 6. 3

long." "Is not this the Carpenter?"

AUGUST 31

1 Pet. 1. 6 and 4. 10: *Manifold temptations: Manifold grace.*

The word "manifold" can be translated "many-coloured". For every temptation there is grace. This is the practical way to use the truth shown in the vision of the Horns and Carpenters. God knows our many-coloured temptations. He has many-coloured grace to meet them—a colour of grace for each temptation of evil. Will you try this plan? Pray instantly for the opposite grace to the temptation that attacks you. There is a carpenter for each horn.

What is your temptation to-day? To despondency? cowardice? unlove? impatience? self-love? Temptations can be manifold. But pouring upon our souls is the sunlight of the grace of God, the many-folded, many-coloured grace; we can take the grace we need: peacefulness that is happiness, courage that is victory, love that never loses hope, patience that is long-suffering with joyfulness, discipline—that which says "No" to self. There is something beyond our understanding in the way our wonderful God makes it possible for us to be that which naturally we are not. But let us leave all that, and in

Heb. 4. 16

simple faith take His many-coloured grace, "grace to help in

Eph. 4. 7

time of need", "according to the measure of the gift of Christ", and that is immeasurable.

SEPTEMBER 1

More than (1)

Psa. 4. 7 : *Thou hast put gladness in my heart, more than in the time that their corn and their wine increased.*

Psalms 3 and 4 were written when David fled from Absalom; and if, as some think, Psalm 4 was written at the time of the Feast of Tabernacles, the harvest and the vintage were over, and the rich stores of corn and new wine were at Absalom's disposal, while David had nothing or very little. It was in every way a hard time for David, and it was not surprising that many said there was "no help for him in God" and "Who will show us any good?" We all know times of trial when the voices within and without talk like that. But David's faith breaks through, and he can honestly say, Thou hast put gladness in my heart *more than* when corn and wine increased. It is not difficult to have gladness in our hearts when we have what we want—corn and wine may stand for whatever we most enjoy doing or possessing—but God asks for something far more than this. He wants what David offered Him when he wrote those words *more than*.

Psa. 3. 2
Psa. 4. 6

SEPTEMBER 2

More than (2)

What David offered to his God was a heart that was utterly satisfied with His will. There were no private reservations, no little whispered "if"—if only I can be where I want to be, and have what I want to have, *then* there will be gladness in my heart, O God; he did not say that—he did not even say, By Thy grace I am glad, I am as glad as I should be if I had those stores of corn and wine. He went further, he flew right out of all the restricting thoughts that might have caged his spirit, up and

125

up into the free air of God, and he said, Thou hast put a new
kind of gladness in my heart. It does not depend on what I
have, it is *more than* that sort of gladness. It is a joy that is
entirely independent of circumstances.

SEPTEMBER 3

More than (3)

How can we reach the place where we can say "More than"?
Have you noticed that, from the place where you stand,
there is always a shining way on the water, in the sunrise or sunset, or in moonlight, or when a bright planet like Venus is rising
or setting? There may be a hundred people on the shore, and
yet each one sees that path beginning just where he or she
stands. I shall never forget my astonishment when I saw this for
the first time.

It is like that with the Bible. Wherever you are reading you
will find a path that leads you from that place straight to the
heart of God, and the desires of God.

SEPTEMBER 4

More than (4)

Perhaps some are puzzled about the path which I said leads
straight from whatever part of the Bible you are reading, to the
heart of God, just as the shining path on the water leads from
the place where your feet are standing across to the other side.

I was reading the Psalms, especially Psalms 3 and 4, when
I wrote that, so I will take these as our starting point—the
place on the shore where we are standing.

In both Psalms there is that clear honesty in prayer that we
find in all Bible prayers. David was not thinking of making the
kind of prayer people would talk about, and call beautiful or
earnest or anything of that sort. He was keen to tell his God
the truth about things, as far as he knew it, even about the
miserable noise of words—a thing that very advanced
Christians would have told him he really ought not to mind at
all. Then there was a restful committal of things in general and

all that unkind talk in particular, and then the will to trust and not be afraid; and as the fears rolled up, prayer again, honest prayer.

I want to remind myself and you that we never get anywhere if we only *look* at the shining path.

SEPTEMBER 5

More than (5)

These notes will have been entirely useless if they have not helped to bring us to the place where our happiness does not depend on the work we are doing, the place we are in, our friends, our health, whether people notice us or not, praise us or not, understand us or not. No single one of the circumstances has any power in itself to upset the joy of God, but it can instantly and utterly quench it if we look at the circumstances instead of up into the Face of light and love that is looking down upon us—the Face of our own God.

This is the shining path, stretching away from the place where we stand to-day to the very heart of God. This is the shining path that shineth more and more as we walk in it.

Prov. 4. 18

SEPTEMBER 6

More and more

2 Cor. 4. 17, 18: R.V. *Our light affliction, which is for the moment, worketh for us more and more exceedingly an eternal weight of glory; while we look not at the things which are seen, but at the things which are not seen.*

There is just a shade of difference between the Authorized and Revised Versions here, but it brings out a wonderful thought. The trial of our faith (whatever it may be) works *more and more*, while we look not *at* it, but *away* from it to that which lies beyond. It does not merely work, it works *more and more* as the days pass and the trial goes on becoming harder to bear, and the things which are seen try to distract us from the things which are not seen. But that "more and more" depends on the *while*. "*While* we look not at . . . but at . . ."

v. 18

SEPTEMBER 7

Psa. 76. 4 : LXX. *Thou dost wonderfully shine forth from the everlasting mountains.*

Sometimes it is dull weather in our soul. Here is a word for such days. Often when it is misty on the plains it is bright on the mountains. "Thou art more glorious and excellent than the mountains" is a lovely word, I think, but this beautiful LXX rendering, which our Lord must often have read, carries us even further. The mist may lie low on the plains, but there is a shining forth from the mountains.

Psa. 36. 5, 6   There is nothing in me. I may be as dull as the plains are when the mist is heavy upon them, but what does that matter? "Thy mercy, O Lord, is in the heavens; and Thy faithfulness reacheth unto the clouds. Thy righteousness is like the great mountains", and from those everlasting mountains "Thou dost wonderfully shine forth".

In dull weather learn to look up to the mountains. Refuse to look down at the plains.

SEPTEMBER 8

This came and I pass it on, thinking that perhaps, by the kindness of the Lord, it may help someone else.

> Great Son of Man, Who walked our dust,
>   Thy love will not forget
> The power the temporal has to thrust
>   And overset.
>
> O let Thy touch make things we see
>   Transparent to our eyes,
> That secrets of Eternity
>   We may surprise.
>
> And let the things which are not seen
>   Shine like the stars at night,
> Till all the space that lies between
>   Be filled with light.

SEPTEMBER 9

Heb. 11. 1 : *Things not seen . . .*
Heb. 11. 27 : *As seeing Him . . .*

There is more to see in this chapter every time one reads it. To-day the chief thought with me is the power that the Unseen had on the lives of those mentioned here. They heard the voice of their God, or in some way not told us, were caused to know what He wanted done. There was nothing visible to help them, and nearly always there was much to go through that must have been very hard for flesh to bear; but to each it was given to go on, to endure, as seeing Him Who is invisible.

They were caused to hear, and caused to know, and taught how to do the will of their God. Things *not seen* mattered more to them than things *seen*. So in this chapter we have battle stories, pilgrim stories, martyr stories and stories of long walks with God; and each one who fought the fight, lived the pilgrim life, and walked the patient walk, began by looking, not at the seen, but at the Unseen. "For the things which are seen are temporal; but the things which are not seen are eternal", and does not the Eternal matter more than anything of time ever can? 2 Cor. 4. 18

SEPTEMBER 10

Heb. 12. 2 : *Looking away from all on earth unto Jesus.*

"Not only at the first moment, but constantly through the whole struggle . . . Christ is always near and in sight." "Consider Him that endured . . . that ye fail not through weariness". "If the Leader bears the brunt of the battle the soldier can follow." And then a warning : "The final failure comes from continuous weakening."

These notes from Westcott have often been God's word to me. I have again and again been brought up to this truth; never once in the Gospels, the Epistles, or the Book of Revelation, is the Christian life regarded as something in any way naturally easy; everywhere we see the symbol that stands for what is stern, deep-cutting, inexorable. The Cross is no play-thing. But "If the leader bears the brunt of the battle the soldier can follow."

SEPTEMBER 11

Matt. 21. 21 : *Jesus answered and said unto them, Verily I
say unto you, If ye have faith, and doubt not, ye
shall not only do this which is done to the fig tree,
but also if ye shall say unto this mountain, Be thou
removed, and be thou cast into the sea; it shall be
done.*

This mountain. What mountain? What does "this mountain" mean to me to-day? I have been thinking of this, and
several mountains seem to me to be in much need of removal.
Oh, to see them cast into the sea, to see them sink like stones
there and never reappear! Sometimes our mountains seem to
be removed—"Be thou removed", we said in earnest prayer,
together or alone; and they did indeed appear to be transported
bodily, and to fall with a glorious splash into the sea; and then
it was as though they were made of cork or some such substance, for we had no sooner rejoiced over their disappearance,
than they reappeared as solid as ever, and sat down where
they were before.

Heb. 10. 36   "Ye have need of patience, that, after ye have done the will
of God, ye might receive the promise." The will of God most
clearly is prayer and continuance in prayer. (There would be
no need of continuance or of patience if mountains had not this
Luke 18. 1 Weym. habit of reappearing.) God give it to us always to "pray and
Heb. 10. 35 never lose heart". "Cast not away therefore your confidence,
which hath great recompense of reward."

SEPTEMBER 12

Prov. 14. 17 : LXX. *A sensible man bears up under many
things.*

There are days when all sorts of things go wrong one after
the other; I expect some of you know what such days are like,
and also the temptation to feel you cannot bear up under anything more.

At such times a plain word like this can help very much; it is
so matter-of-fact and unfussy. Take it or leave it, it seems to say,
there is the fact: "A sensible man bears up under many
things."

But often we want something that goes deeper. Here is the word then: "Consider Him that endured such contradiction of sinners against Himself, lest ye be wearied and faint in your minds." Heb. 12. 3

SEPTEMBER 13

Psa. 18. 30: *As for God, His way is perfect.*

God is love, so we may change the word and say, As for Love, His way is perfect. This has been helping me.

One of the ways of Love is to prepare us beforehand for any hard thing that He knows is near. Perhaps this word will be His loving preparation to some heart for a disappointment, or for some trial of faith, something known to others, or some secret sorrow between the Father and His child. As for Love, His way is perfect.

SEPTEMBER 14

Have you ever noticed, you who read the Psalms for the day, that in the middle of the month two verses come together which show us the two sides of life and the ways of our God with us? One side is perplexing, unexplained, full of mystery, perhaps painful mystery. The other is simple and glad; a child can understand it.

"Thy way is in the sea [who ever saw a way in the sea?], and Thy paths in the great waters [where no path is] : and Thy footsteps are not known." Feet walking on water was (I read somewhere) the Egyptian symbol for the impossible. And then, "Thou leddest Thy people like sheep:" Shepherd-love, Shepherd-care, Shepherd-tenderness. It has often helped me in the middle of a difficult month to think of these great pictures laid alongside in this Psalm. Psa. 77. 19 P.B.V. v. 20

SEPTEMBER 15

Matt. 11. 26 : *Even so, Father: for so it seemed good in Thy sight.*

"Even so, Father" in Aramaic is, "O yes, my Father, for such is Your will"—the"Yes" of complete content, the welcoming "Yes" of acceptance. He asks us: *Are you pleased with My*

will?—not, Are you going to bear up under it and not show
your real feelings?

We all know what it is to plan a pleasure for a child and
then watch to see its pleasure. Some of us know what it is to
plan the best our love can think of, which yet may be,
naturally speaking, a disappointment to that child; and we
know how we watch for its response. Love is planning for us.
Love has planned the best that Love could plan. Perhaps we
cannot help one another more than by praying that we may
never disappoint our Father's faith in us, but always follow our
blessed Lord in this as in everything, and answer His trust with
the words "O yes, Father." "*Are you pleased with My will,
My child?*" "*O yes, my Father.*"

SEPTEMBER 16

Acts 27. 25 : *I believe God, that it shall be even as it was told
me.*

There is nearly always something deep in our hearts about
which some special word has been told us by our Lord, or
about which we have some inward assurance that we know
is from Him. It is this that Satan assaults. He tries, by under-
mining our confidence, to get us out of peace into fear. Of all
the answers to such suggestions as those which he is sure to
make, there are none more certain to conquer than this, "I
believe God, that it shall be even as it was told me."

SEPTEMBER 17

Psa. 106. 12, 13 : *They believed His words;
They sang His praises.
They soon forgat His works.*

Have you ever known a weakening in the inward places of
your soul because you had let slip the memory of what your
God did in the past? You had believed His words, you had
sung His praises, for in very truth you had seen His words
fulfilled. And then, somehow, the memory faded, blotted out
by a disappointment perhaps, and you "forgat His works."

I have known this happen, and I have proved that after such
forgetfulness prayer becomes less adventurous, less brave in

faith and expectation. We ask for the smaller rather than the greater things, and then (as in the story from which I am quoting) "leanness" enters into the soul. *v.* 15

May the Lord, by His Spirit, quicken our memories, and help us to do our part by gathering up the forces of memory. It is worthwhile to do anything that will help us to this. "We Song of S. 1. 4 will remember Thy love" and all the way the Lord our God See Deut. 8. 2 has led us.

SEPTEMBER 18

Phil. 1. 6 : *He Which hath begun a good work in you will perform it until the day of Jesus Christ.*

To-day I have found something fresh in this—"He Which hath begun a good work . . . will perform it until the Day of Jesus Christ"—will go on to perform it in preparation for the Day of Christ. So often some fervent loving prayer for another has not seen its hopes fulfilled. But "He Which hath begun . . ."; may it not be that there has been a beginning, deep in that soul, unknown perhaps to itself? I have often found later on that it has been so. Even though we never know, it does not matter. Of one thing we are sure : prayer is heard; prayer is answered; forces are set in motion by prayer in the Name of our Lord Jesus which will not cease, but will continue until that which has been begun is perfected. Love will perfect that which it begins. It will not forsake the work of See Psa. 138. 8 its own hands.

SEPTEMBER 19

Mark 16. 4 : R.V. *And looking up, they see that the stone is rolled back: for it was exceeding great.*

Sometimes the Revised Version gives a new ray of light. I found one here : "And looking up, they see". The sorrowful women were looking down as they walked. We often do that in sorrow. They were wondering who would roll away the stone. They did not see *till they looked up* that it had been rolled away. We do not always see the stones that are exceeding great rolled back the moment we look up, but "Cast not away . . . Heb. 10. 35 your confidence," you who are, as it seems, looking up in vain.

It "hath great recompense of reward." Only be sure not to look down or even too much at the stone. *Look up.*

SEPTEMBER 20

The thoughts of God

Think through me, thoughts of God, when I have to deal with difficult souls. Let me see in each soul an opportunity to claim the powers of Calvary. Love through me, Love of God, love that hard soul through me. Flow through me, Patience of God, flow over the roughness of that soul even as the sea flows over the rough rocks. Hope through me, Hope of God. O God of Hope, hope afresh in me as I touch that soul again. Let me not remember past disappointments. Let me begin each morning with hope, as Thou dost begin each morning with hope for me, even me.

> For love, brave love that ventureth,
>   For love that faileth not I come,
> For love that never wearieth,
>   Nor findeth burdens burdensome.
>
> I come for hope that springeth green,
>   And burneth steadfast like a star;
> For faith that pierceth through the seen
>   To things eternal, things that are.
>
> O Love, that lightenest all my ways,
>   Within, without, below, above,
> Flow through the minutes of my days,
>   The sum of all my life be love.

SEPTEMBER 21

2 Cor. 10. 1: (Weymouth) *The gentleness and self-forgetful-ness of Christ.*

I cannot tell you how often these words have helped me when I had a difficult letter to write—Paul was in the middle of that sort of letter then; or when I had to explain something to someone who seemed unable to understand—his position at that moment.

It is so easy to let the "I" slip in, so easy to be hard in spirit, if one is up against unfairness, misrepresentation, misunderstanding of any sort, as Paul was then. But there is the thought of the gentleness of the Lord Jesus, and His self-forgetfulness.

May He remind us of Himself in moments of temptation, and may we be near enough to be reminded.

SEPTEMBER 22

2 Cor. 2. 15 : *We are unto God a sweet savour of Christ.*

Literally, "Christ's fragrance am I, unto God." (Conybeare.) Paul is speaking of the fragrance of the incense carried in the Triumph of a Roman Emperor, to illustrate God's triumph over His enemies. We are as captives following in Christ's triumphal procession, yet at the same time His incense-bearers, those who are unto God a sweet savour of Christ.

Whatever we have to offer owes everything to that which causes it to be (without Me ye can do *nothing*); yet God counts it as something. He even thinks of us as fragrance : "Christ's fragrance am I, unto God." I think it is very wonderful.

SEPTEMBER 23

Song of Songs 4. 12, 15 : *A garden inclosed . . . a spring shut up, a fountain sealed . . . a fountain of gardens, . . . and streams from Lebanon.*

> Lord, make of this our pleasant field
> A garden cool and shadowy,
> A spring shut up, a fountain sealed
> For Thee, Lord Jesus, only Thee.
>
> And as from far untrodden snow
> Of Lebanon the streams run free,
> Dear Lord, command our streams to flow,
> That thirsty men may drink of Thee.

The garden inclosed, the spring shut up, the fountain sealed, describe our hidden life in Christ. If there be not this hidden life, kept like a well shut up for its Owner alone, there will be no fountains of living waters, no streams to flow forth for the refreshing of others. Let us pray this little song from our heart.

SEPTEMBER 24

Deut. 1. 31 : (Rotherham) *Carried . . . until ye came into this place.*

v. 30

Thank God, the Bible words are so simple. Rotherham has "Your God Who is going before you" (like the "He goeth before" of the Shepherd verse) "He shall fight for you". "Thy God carried thee . . . until ye came into this place."

"This place" is different for each of us. For some it is the place of the heart's choice as well as His; for some it is not. For all of us it is a new place each day, and we shall never be there again. I have been thinking of it as an opportunity that will not recur. To lose it is to lose it for ever, and that is a solemn thought. Is it not like our Father to lead up to it by reminding

Isa. 63. 9
Deut. 1. 31

us that He bare us and carried us all the days of old? "As a man doth bear his son" in all the way that we went until we came into this place, He bare us and carried us. The love that we proved yesterday is the same to-day. It will be the same to-morrow. Trusting that love we can go on to-day in "this place".

SEPTEMBER 25

Deut. 4. 7 : *So nigh . . . as the Lord our God is in all things that we call upon Him for.*

Deuteronomy is full of light for all who desire to follow our Lord fully, and does most wonderfully "speak to our condition".

This verse must have helped millions. It came to me yesterday as if read for the first time : "so nigh . . . as the Lord our God is in all things that we call upon Him for"—*in all things,* in this which fills the heart of any one of us to-day.

Those who go amongst the Hindus know how utterly different it is with them. In desolation, bewilderment, need of any kind, they have no God so nigh unto them that they can be sure their prayer is heard.

v. 9

"Lest thou forget". Do we take time to remember? A very busy person was running through his day's life with a Quaker, who listened quietly, and then said, "Friend, when dost thou think?"

"Specially the day that thou stoodest before the Lord thy *vv.* 10-12
God in Horeb, . . . and ye came near and stood . . . and the
Lord spake". Have we not known such days?

SEPTEMBER 26

Psa. 35. 1 :   *Fight against them that fight against me.*
Psa. 35. 3 : (Kay) *Be a barrier against my pursuers.*

What are the things that fight against me? Let us not lose
the comfort and power that is in this word for us by relating
the prayer to the larger things only, it touches the smallest.
The wave that sweeps over the great rock, is the same that
sweeps over the tiny shell on the shore. It is the little things of
life, the minute unimportant-looking things, that are most
likely to shatter our peace; because they are so small that we are
very likely to fight them ourselves, instead of looking up at
once to our Strong God, our Barrier between us and them.
"Close the gate, or bar up the way :— as the cloudy pillar   Exod. 14. 20
formed a barricade between the Egyptians and Israel" is Kay's
note.

Fight against them that fight against me—the feelings, the
little foolish feelings that want to keep us back from saying to
the blessed Will of God "I am content to do it", fight Thou Psa. 40. 10
against them, O God; "and my soul shall be joyful in the   P.B.V.
Lord : it shall rejoice in His salvation . . . Lord, Who is like Psa. 35. 9. 10
unto Thee, Which deliverest the poor from him that is too
strong for him?"

What a joyful life ours is, continually proving His tenderness
in the very little things. There is nothing too small for Him to
help. He is indeed a Barrier between us and our pursuers. How Psa. 36. 7 R.V.
precious is His lovingkindness. Now for a day of joy!

SEPTEMBER 27

Deut. 7. 7, 8 : *Our God did not set His love upon us or choose
us for anything in us, but because the Lord loved
us*—He loves us.

When I was a small child, hard-pushed for a reason as to
why I had done something, I used to fall back on "just
because". So in this great passage of Scripture we have the

child's word, the reason that is no reason. God loves us "just because" He loves. He has taken Him a company from the midst of another company; He loved us for no reason at all except because He loved us. Why? He must have had a special purpose. Have we discovered it? Are we fulfilling it?

John 15. 19

SEPTEMBER 28

Exod. 35. 13 : R.V. mar. *Presence-bread.*

When our Lord Jesus sat at the table of His friends, and took the bread and blessed it and brake it and gave it to them, and was known to them in the breaking of the bread, might they not have thought of it as "Presence-bread"?

Luke 24. 30

What of our meal times? What is there to hinder them from being like that meal? What is there to hinder all our bread from being Presence-bread?

As I thought of this, words came as a sort of Grace, and I used them before my next meal and found that they helped :

> Hallow our meal, dear Lord,
>   This eventide,[1]
> Master beloved, adored,
>   With us abide;
> So from Thy plenitude
>   Shall we be fed,
> And all our common food
>   Be Presence-bread.

SEPTEMBER 29

Rev. 1. 11 : *I am Alpha and Omega, the first and the last.*

What must it have been to hear a great voice, as of a trumpet, saying these words? They are the New Testament echo of that glorious word in the Old Testament, "The Lord will go before you; and the God of Israel will be your rearward."

Isa. 52. 12 R.V.

[1] Or morning-tide.

In Rotherham it is: "For your Van-guard is the Lord, and your Rear-guard the God of Israel." Alpha and Omega—Vanguard and Rearguard. No wonder that over and over again, in one form or another, our Lord says to us, "Fear not", "Let not your heart be troubled, neither let it be afraid." He Who begins, finishes; He Who leads us on, follows behind to deal in love with our poor attempts and our mistakes; to cause His blessed pardon to flow over our sins till they are utterly washed away; and to turn to flight the foe who would pursue after us. He is first and He is last, and we are gathered up between, as in great arms of eternal lovingkindness.

SEPTEMBER 30

Isa. 52. 12 : R.V. *The God of Israel will be your rearward.*

Have you ever looked back over a month and felt more than a little disheartened over the failures and mistakes—the blots on the page you had meant to keep so white?

There is a most beautiful and tender meaning in the word "rearward" which again and again has comforted me. It may be new to some of you. It means *to gather.* The Revised Version margin has, *to gather you up.* An army as it goes forth into new territory needs a Vanguard to protect the van, and a Rearguard to protect the rear, so our glorious God uses these two words in speaking of His loving work to us-ward. The Lord will go before us. Our Vanguard is the Lord. And the Lord God of Israel will be our Rearward—following after, not only to defend us, should the enemy attack in the rear, as he often does, but to gather us up if we flag and are weary because of the way. And if He gathers us up, He gathers up also the things we have dropped, our poor fallen resolutions, mistakes, everything, and deals with them Himself. There is eternal love and tenderness in these dear words, "The Lord God of Israel shall gather you up." Not only that, *The glory of the Lord shall be* Isa. 58. 8 R.V. *thy rearward.*

So, as we travel on into another month we need not fear, Eternal Love is our Vanguard, the glory of Eternal Love is our Rearguard. The everlasting Arms of Everlasting Love shall gather us up.

OCTOBER 1

Dan. 4. 26 : *The Heavens do rule.*

This wonderful sentence puts all that we believe into four words. Again and again during these days it will still our hearts and keep us in the place of peace, if we say them to ourselves and let the power that is in them have its way in us.

"The Heavens do rule." Often when we read history we feel as if hell, not Heaven, ruled this poor world, but that is not true. In spite of all, behind all, above all, the Heavens do rule, and our eyes shall see the victory of Him of Whom it is written, "On His head were many crowns; . . . And He hath on His vesture and on His thigh a name written, KING OF KINGS, AND LORD OF LORDS."

Rev. 19. 12, 16

OCTOBER 2

Job 1. 14 : *And there came a messenger unto Job, . . .*

We know whose messenger he was; and the Lord, Who gave the cruel master leave to send his messenger, was covered in cloud, so that His tormented servant could not find Him anywhere : "I go forward, but He is not there; and backward, but I cannot perceive Him : on the left hand, where He doth work, but I cannot behold Him : He hideth Himself on the right hand, that I cannot see Him : But"––glorious climax––"He knoweth the way that I take : when He hath tried me, I shall come forth as gold." And that was the utmost that the messenger could do. This *"But"* seems to me one of the mountain peaks of the Old Testament story, like the "but" of Dan. 3. 18. *"But if not".*

Job 23. 8-10

With this great story of Job set deep in his heart, and interpreting his own experience, I do not wonder that St Paul recognized "the messenger of Satan" sent to buffet him; the Spirit of God Who inspired the writing of that poem was never

2 Cor. 12. 7, 9, 10

140

far from him. "He made known His ways" unto him, where Fsa. 103. 7 others only saw His acts. St Paul had the comfort of the light on the page of his life, and therefore he was more than a conqueror, able to hear his dear Lord's reply to his prayer, able to tell it to us, able to write : "And we know that all things Rom. 8. 28 work together for good to them that love God".

And if we, who have not only the story of Job, but also the story of Paul before us, fail in faith, or peace, or courage, must it not cause the angels to wonder, knowing it need not be so? This has come home to me very much of late. But we need not fail : "In all these things we are more than conquerors through Rom. 8. 37 Him that loved us."

OCTOBER 3

Some find it hard to believe that Satan (a conquered foe) can interfere in the affairs of a child of God. Yet we read of St Paul earnestly endeavouring to do something and Satan 1 Thess. 2. 18 hindering him. The reason for Satan's power was not prayerlessness. "Night and day am I praying with passionate earnestness 1 Thess. 3. 10
Way that I may see your faces". Satan could not touch his spirit, his heart's affections, or any other vital thing in him, but he could so order events that the apostle could not do for these children of his love all that he longed to do. He could only write letters. He could not be with them.

And in the familiar 2 Cor. 12. 7, we have a still stranger thing, a messenger from Satan allowed to do bodily hurt, and allowed to continue to hurt, we are not told for how long.

So it is clear that there are activities in the Unseen which are not explained to us. Every now and then the curtain between is drawn aside for a moment, and we see. But it is soon drawn back again.

Only this we know : "When I called upon Thee, Thou Psa. 138. 3
P.B.V. heardest me; and enduedst my soul with much strength." If that be so what does anything matter? Oh, to use all disappointments, delays and trials of faith and patience as St Paul used his. What golden gain came to our glorious Lord because of these experiences. And see how he closes this letter to the Thessalonians which is so full of human longing: "The very God of peace sanctify you wholly: and I pray God your whole

1 Thess.
5. 23, 24
spirit and soul and body be preserved blameless unto the coming of our Lord Jesus Christ. Faithful is He that calleth you, Who also will do it." He will do all I long to do and cannot, *Faithful is He: He will do it.*

OCTOBER 4

Eph. 6. 16 : R.V. *The shield of faith, wherewith ye shall be able to quench all the fiery darts of the evil one.*

The word used for shield signifies a great oblong shield which covers the whole body, and the dart mentioned here is the kind which when it strikes a hard object catches fire. The promise is that when the dart strikes the great shield of faith, though it is set on fire, it is quenched. It cannot pierce the shield. It cannot burn the one who is behind the shield. The promise covers all manner of darts. The kind of dart hurled against us makes no difference to the promise. "All" means *all*. Do we expect "all" to mean *all*? Is there a secret fear in our hearts about a certain kind of temptation which perhaps we shall not be able to overcome? Away with this fear! It is of the devil. The shield of faith is ready to be taken up and used. If we take it up and use it, not a single dart of any sort will pierce it. *All means all.*

OCTOBER 5

Mark 4. 38 : *And He was in the hinder part of the ship, asleep on a pillow: and they awake Him, and say unto Him, Master, carest Thou not that we perish?*
Zeph. 3. 17 : *The Lord thy God is in the midst of thee . . .*
and mar.   *He will rest in His love—be silent in His love.*

We know that the disciples need not have been afraid, they need not have disturbed our Lord's rest; but something I had never thought of before came to me yesterday, as I pictured that tossing boat and those frightened men and the resting Lord. Do we never do just what they did? He is resting in His love, in the silence of love. Do not we, His lovers, sometimes break into the sweetness of that silence with a fear, a cry that is almost "Carest Thou not?"

No one paragraph, even in our Bible, shows life as a whole. There are other aspects, I know, but this, which is perhaps the very innermost—the heart of the heart of love—is something we are meant to look at often, and far more, *to live*.

There is a silence which can be only met by silence. "Silence is not a gap to be filled. It is the greatest of all preparations, and the climax of all adoration."[1]

> *He will be silent in His love.*
> *Surely towards God silence becometh my soul,*
> *Surely towards God be thou silent, my soul.*

Zeph. 3. 17 mar.
Psa. 62. 1. 5 Rotherham

Let the storm beat as it will outside; within, let there be peace, so that undisturbed He may rest in His love.

And now this translation which is quite fresh to me: "He will renew thee with His love". Are they not dear words? "He will rest in His love". "He will renew thee with His love".

LXX mar.

OCTOBER 6

> Thou art my Lord Who slept upon the pillow,
>   Thou art my Lord Who calmed the furious sea;
> What matter beating wind and tossing billow
>   If only we are in the boat with Thee?
>
> Hold us in quiet through the age-long minute
>   While Thou art silent and the wind is shrill;
> What boat can sink when Thou, dear Lord, art in it?
>   What heart can faint that resteth on Thy will?

OCTOBER 7

Psa. 107. 29, 30: *He maketh the storm a calm, so that the waves thereof are still. Then are they glad because they be quiet; so He bringeth them unto their desired haven.*

"Then are they glad because they be quiet;" the words were music to me. Then, in reading the different stories of the Lord calming the sea, I found this: "He cometh . . . and would have

Mark 6. 48

[1] *The Fellowship of Silence*, by various authors, edited by the Rev. Cecil Hepher.

Weym., Roth passed by them"—"as if intending to pass them"—"and was wishing to pass by them". The more literal the translation, the more startling it is.

As I pondered the matter I saw that this "age-long minute" was part of the spiritual preparation of these men for a life that at that time was unimagined by them—a life of dauntless faith and witness in the absence of any manifestation of the power of their Lord; and it must be the same to-day. Such minutes must be in our lives, unless our training is to be unlike that of every saint and warrior who ever lived. Our "minute"

Psa. 13. 1   may seem endless—"How long wilt Thou forget me," cried David out of the depths of his—but perhaps looking back we shall see in such an experience a great and shining opportunity. Words are spoken then that are spoken at no other time, such

Matt. 11. 6 as the immortal words to John the Baptist, "And blessed is he, whosoever shall not be offended in Me." We have a chance to prove our glorious God, to prove that His joy is strength and that His peace passeth all understanding, and to know the love of Christ that passeth knowledge.

And the "minute" always ends in one way, there is no other

Mark 6. 50 ending recorded anywhere: "He talked with them, and saith unto them, Be of good cheer: It is I; be not afraid . . . and the wind ceased."

Psa. 107. 30 "Then are they glad because they be quiet; so He bringeth them unto their desired haven."

OCTOBER 8

Rom. 15. 13 : *The God of hope fill you with all joy and peace in believing, that ye may abound in hope, through the power of the Holy Ghost.*

These words have often helped us to go on hoping for those who were disappointing us. But this morning they came differently to me.

Luke 22. 28   "Ye are they which have continued with Me in My
Matt. 26. 40 temptations." A few hours later—"Could ye not watch with
Matt. 26. 56 Me one hour?" Very soon after—"All the disciples forsook Him, and fled."

John 17. 6   "They have kept Thy word" . . . "There was also a strife
Luke 22. 24   among them, which of them should be accounted the greatest"

—this had happened only a little while before. And yet, so perfect was the understanding between Father and Son that He does not explain—to the all-knowing Father the all-knowing Son says, "They have kept Thy word". How *could* He say it? What does it mean to us? Just this: Our Lord of Love, our blessed Lord Jesus, looks upon us with such loving eyes that He sees us as we are in our deepest, lowliest, holiest moments, in those hours when, like John, we lean upon His bosom, and He speaks to us, and we all but see His face.

He knows, as no one else can know, the deep longing of our hearts. He knows, as no one else can know, how far we fall. "Not as though I had already attained"—He knows that; but "I press on"—He knows that, too.

Phil. 3. 12

v. 15 R.V.

The love of the Father has the same golden quality of hope. "The God of Hope" hopes for us, even for us. He never loses hope. He accepted the word of His beloved Son: "They have kept [intently observed] Thy word", in spite of times when they had seemed most grievously to disregard it—when for example at our Lord's own table they strove about the dreadful matter of pre-eminence. The God of Hope saw what they wished to be, what they yet would be. And He looks at us like that. Is there not something in this that touches us to the quick? How grieve a love like that? And is there not encouragement, too, for the strengthening of our souls?

OCTOBER 9

1 John 4. 16 : (Rotherham) *We have come to understand and to trust the love which God hath in us.*

I have been thinking much of this translation. We can never fully understand that love, but we can begin to understand it even here and now, and as we understand, we trust. This means that we trust all that the love of God does; all He gives, and all He does not give; all He says, and all He does not say. To it all we say, by His loving enabling, I *trust*. Let us be content with our Lord's will, and tell Him so, and not disappoint Him by wishing for anything He does not give. The more we understand His love, the more we trust.

OCTOBER 10

Rom. 8. 37 :   *More than conquerors.*
Jas. 1. 2 : R.V. *Count it all joy . . . when ye fall into manifold temptations.*

Sometimes when we read the words of those who have been more than conquerors, we feel almost despondent. "I shall never be like that", we feel. But they won through, step by step; by little acts of will, little denials of self, little inward victories, by faithfulness in very little things, they became what they are. No one sees these little hidden steps, they only see the accomplishment; but even so, those small steps were taken. There is no sudden triumph, no spiritual maturity that is the work of a moment. So let us all take courage; not one of us is too weak to be made more than a conqueror.

Jas. 1. 2

Pastor Monod, in speaking of "Count it all joy", uses the illustration of a man whose physical force is developed by carrying heavy burdens. He takes the words of the Apostle James to mean that there is something in trial which God uses to perfect strength : "Let us leave God to do His own work. He will not allow us to suffer in vain."

OCTOBER 11

Ride forth singing.
If thou hast a fearful thought, share it not with a weakling, whisper it to thy saddle-bow, and ride forth singing.
                                    King Alfred the Great.

Have I fear that Thou dost know?
Fear of weakness, fear of failing
(Though Thy power is all prevailing);
Or a haunting fear of bringing
Care to others?
Share it not with a weakling,
Whisper it to thy saddle-bow,
And ride forth singing.

Many fears can murmur low,
Fear of ills the future holdeth
(Though indeed Thy grace upholdeth),
Dulling fear and fear sharp-stinging,
Fear that tortures;
Share it not with a weakling,
Whisper it to thy saddle-bow,
And ride forth singing.

OCTOBER 12

2 Sam. 2. 7 : mar. *Sons of valour.*

Can you find a promise that if we follow the Lord Jesus
Christ, life is going to be fairly easy? I do not think we shall
find even one. But we shall find ever so many promises assuring
us that however things are, we may count on strength to make
us brave, and peace to keep our hearts at rest.

Because this is so, our Lord and Captain expects us to be
"sons of valour", as the word translated "valiant" in the Old
Testament means. And He is saying to each of us what King
David said long ago to his friends, "Now let your hands be
strengthened and be ye valiant"—be ye sons of valour.

OCTOBER 13

There are countless promises given to us for times when
things are hard. There is one in the Old Testament which,
perhaps lest we should be tempted to fear that it was spoken
only or specially to Joshua, the writer of a New Testament
book quotes as if spoken to himself and to all who read his
writings : "I will never leave thee, nor forsake thee. So that we
may boldly say, The Lord is my helper". I like that "boldly",
don't you? We are not meant to shiver when faced by
temptations, we may look up to Him Who conquered the
powers of evil when He "reigned from the Tree." They can
never say He did not, for He made a shew of them openly. We
follow a triumphant Christ, and if upon Him is all our reliance,
we need never be defeated. To-day, from hour to hour, if we
look to Him, He can and He will lead us on in triumph.

Josh. 1. 5

Heb. 13. 5, 6

Psa. 96. 10
Jerome

And if something has to be done that seems quite impossible, the same certainty holds good. Over and over again I have seen the Lord do "impossible" things. I think He delights in the impossible, and He delights to meet the faith of one who looks up to Him and says, Lord, Thou knowest I cannot, but I believe Thou canst.

OCTOBER 14

Have you ever thought how infectious fear can be? It spreads from one to another more quickly and certainly than any of the fevers we know so well. So, for the sake of others, let us refuse the spirit of fear which God never gives us (if He does not, who does?), and let us open our hearts wide to the Spirit "of power and love and discipline." We can do this if we will.

2 Tim. 1. 7 R.V.

Thank God, courage is as infectious as discouragement. Have you not often felt the cheer and strength that seem to flow from one whose mind is stayed on God? I have.

And I have been thinking of another, a greater, reason for refusing the spirit of fear. When we are downhearted, or fearful, or weak, we are saying to everybody, by looks and by deeds if not by words, After all, our Lord is not to be absolutely trusted. Somewhere near us, though we do not see them, are others, the good angels and the spirits of evil. To them, too, when we yield to fear, we say the same dishonouring thing. So for the greater glory of our glorious Saviour Who has never once failed us, and never will fail us, Who has loved and led and guarded us all these years, let us look to Him now and pray from the ground of our heart, Lord, give us valour.

OCTOBER 15

Heb. 13. 5 : *I will never leave thee, nor forsake thee.*

Many years ago someone told me that "forsake" is a compound of three words in the Greek, "leave behind in". It conveys the thought of leaving comrades exposed to peril in the conflict, or forsaking them in some crisis of danger. Westcott interprets this verse, "I will in no wise desert you or leave you alone in the field of contest, or in a position of suffering, I will in no wise let go—loose hold—my sustaining grasp."

This promise cannot fail. Let us stand upon it, and rejoice in it; and in times of trial let us show to all who observe us that these words are for ever true: Christ our Lord is with us, Alleluia. From all fearing, from all weakening, from all turning back, the Lord deliver us, that standing fast in one Spirit, strong in the Lord and in the power of His might, we may be "to the praise of the glory of His grace".   Eph. 1. 6

OCTOBER 16

Little prayers

Sometimes we are very much disappointed with ourselves because we cannot pray proper prayers, only little ones that hardly seem to be prayers at all. I have been finding much comfort in the little prayers of the Gospels. They could not be more little.

There was Peter's, "Lord, save me", and the poor mother's,   Matt. 14. 30
"Lord, help me"; and sometimes even less, no prayer at all but   Matt. 15. 25
only the briefest telling of the trouble, "My servant lieth at   Matt. 8. 6
home sick"; and less than that, a thought, and a touch, "She   Matt. 9. 21
said within herself, If I may but touch . . ."

Again we hear of just a feeling, "They were troubled", and a   Matt. 14. 26
cry, "They cried out for fear"—that was all, but it was enough.

Often in the throng of the day's work and warfare, there will not be time for more than a very little prayer—a thought, a touch, a feeling, a cry—but it is enough; so tender, so near, is the love of our Lord.

OCTOBER 17

Psa. 119. 173 : *Let Thine hand help me.*

This little prayer has often been mine. These short Bible prayers are just what we want in days when we are tired or hard-pressed, so I pass this one on for those who need it. You will find it enough. It is like the touch on the electric light switch—just a touch, and the power comes flowing from the power-house—the power that turns to light.

OCTOBER 18

Gen. 15. 2 : *Lord God, what wilt Thou give me?*

When thinking of the further reaches of prayer I came on this, the simplest of all, like the words of a small child before it has learnt not to ask for things for itself. If the friend of God could speak so to his God, we may in all simplicity do so too. "Lord God, what wilt Thou give me?"

Just as a child passes from the less to the greater in desire, so we find in our Bible that the desire of man, as he walks further on with God, grows and grows till we come to such words as Paul's, words that reach far beyond any earthly good—"That I may know Him, and the power of His resurrection, and the fellowship of His sufferings"; and soon that other word follows, so often forgotten in hurried prayer : the first good thing promised is not the thing for which we prayed, but *peace.*

Phil. 3. 10

"Lord God, what wilt Thou give me?"

"The peace of God, which passeth all understanding, shall keep your hearts and minds through Christ Jesus." Is not peace an answer?

Phil. 4. 7

OCTOBER 19

Psa. 141. 2 : *Let my prayer be set forth before Thee as incense; and the lifting up of my hands as the evening sacrifice.*

When vision fadeth, and the sense of things,
  And powers dissolve like colours in the air,
And no more can I bring Thee offerings,
  Nor any ordered prayer,

Then, like a wind blowing from Paradise,
  Falleth a healing word upon mine ear,
Let the lifting up of my hands be as the evening
  sacrifice;
The Lord doth hear.

OCTOBER 20

This morning I read the Smyrna Letter and found that the word "tribulation" in Rev. 2. 9 means the pressure of the stones that grind the wheat, or that force the juice out of the grape.

The making of Bread and Wine, nothing less, is the purpose of that pressure; and He Who weighs the winds measures the force of the pressure. Of this we can be sure. What about our prayers for those who are under pressure? Are they of the earth, earthy, or are they Heavenly in quality?

How often have I found myself asking for relief for those I love, just simple blessed relief from the grinding pressure of the stones; but would not another, a braver, deeper kind of prayer help them far more?

Bread and Wine—the very words are hallowed. Let us pray alongside our Lord as He makes of mortal souls, through pressure, something that will be used for the life of the world, Bread and Wine.

OCTOBER 21

The "Even there" of Psalm 139. 10 this morning took me to the Lord's "Even so" of Matthew 11. 26.

In Psalm 86. 11 we have the prayer that we all pray, "Teach me Thy way, O Lord;" and Rotherham has it, "Point out to me Thy way," as if there were several possible ways and, fearing lest we should mistake His directions, we said, as a child might to his father, "Please point."

Then He points perhaps to something very unexpected, and for a moment we are bewildered; then, "Even there shall Thy hand lead me, and Thy right hand shall hold me." *Even there*.

And our Lord's "Even so, Father: for so it seemed good in Thy sight", carries a deeper meaning in Aramaic: *even so* means *yes*. "Yes, Father; for so it seemed good in Thy sight." What words of peace for us to-day and every day: *Even there; Even so—yes, Father*. Luke 10. 21

OCTOBER 22

John 20. 19 : *When the doors were shut*

Often our thoughts are like a crowd of people talking together in a room whose doors are shut, and because of the setting of some hope that had a bright sunrise, it is a sorrowful time.

There may be love, understanding love, all round us, and yet we may be needing some word of life in our own soul, something that would do what only the Divine can do. "Lord, to whom shall we go? Thou hast the words of eternal life."

John 6. 68

One day lately, when feeling like this, I took my New Testament, and it opened of itself at John 20, and the first words I read were these: "The same day at evening . . . when the doors were shut . . . came Jesus and stood in the midst, and saith . . . Peace be unto you. And when He had so said, He shewed unto them His hands and His side." It is all there—the shut doors (for we cannot say aloud all that fills our mind), the dreary evening, then the risen Lord, and peace.

OCTOBER 23

Is it not always so? Does He not come just when He is needed most, and is not His first word always, Peace be unto you? "Jesus Christ the same yesterday, and to-day, and for ever."

John 20. 19
Heb. 13. 8

John 20. 20
Luke 24. 40

I wonder if He showed them His hands and His side, and His feet, too, not only that they might recognize Him in their ill-lighted room, but that always on to the end they might remember this: I, Whom you follow, suffered; if you would follow Me you cannot avoid suffering; you must not be surprised at any suffering. "Think it not strange", "Count it all joy". More even than that (for His call all along had been to take up the cross and carry it), it seems to me that by His showing of hands and side and feet, He was impressing this great truth upon their minds: "Verily, verily, I say unto you, Except a corn of wheat fall into the ground and die, it abideth alone: but if it die, it bringeth forth much fruit." "There is no life except by death". But first He said, "Peace be unto you."

1 Pet. 4. 12
Jas. 1. 2

John 12. 24

OCTOBER 24

2 Chron. 8. 12, 13 R.V. *Burnt offerings . . . even as the duty of every day required.*

Sometimes we look ahead and things look rather difficult, indeed impossible. But we have nothing to do with to-morrow, we have only to think about to-day; and the one thing that matters is that we offer our burnt offering (all we have to give of time, strength, love, everything) as the duty of the day requires.

OCTOBER 25

2 Chron. 29. 27, 28 : *And when the burnt offering began, the song of the Lord began also with the trumpets, and with the instruments ordained by David King of Israel . . . And all this continued until the burnt offering was finished.*

What a picture of offering our all with joy and "not grudgingly [that is, with an inward wish that it was not so], or of necessity [that is, because we must], for God loveth a cheerful giver." 2 Cor. 9. 7

What is your burnt offering? God knows and you know. Whatever it be, offer it with a song. Do not stop half-way through. "And all this continued until the burnt offering was finished."

OCTOBER 26

Lev. 6. 12, 13 : *The fire upon the altar shall be burning in it; it shall not be put out . . . The fire shall ever be burning upon the altar; it shall never go out.*
Exod. 30. 7, 8 : *Sweet incense every morning . . . a perpetual incense.*
2 Thess. 3. 16 : *Peace always.*

I have noticed that often the first thing attacked is peace. (I suppose in earthly war, the sentinel is likely to be the first to be put out of action if possible, and Peace is our sentinel.) When our peace is shattered, vital prayer ceases, and the love which was to burn and not be put out—the love that finds sheer joy in sacrifice—fails utterly. So let us guard our peace. In disturbed times we can learn that circumstances have no power whatever over peace : "When He giveth quietness, who then [what then] can make trouble?" The only thing that has power to do that is sin. "Vouchsafe, O Lord, to keep us this day without sin." Job. 34. 29

OCTOBER 27

John 21. 17 : *Lord, Thou knowest all things;*
Thou knowest that I love Thee.

And to that word have we not often heard Him answer
softly in our hearts, Yes, I know. Something like that I found in
a small Psalm at the end of the book of Psalms in the LXX.[1] A
note says it is a genuine one of David. As the Septuagint "is the
earliest version of the Old Testament Scriptures of which we
possess any certain knowledge", and as we find it constantly
quoted by the New Testament writers, we may, I think, trust a
note like this, and think of the little extra Psalm as David's own.
I am glad that we have it, for I found something very dear and
human in it. David has been speaking of how he made a
musical instrument and tuned it with his fingers, and then, as
though realizing what a trifle it was after all, he says, "And
who shall tell my Lord?" Back comes the instant answer, or
that certainty of heart which is an answer: "The Lord
Himself, He Himself hears."

Have we not found a joy in doing some little thing for love
of Him, something quite small and inconspicuous, of no value
except as done for Him, and then suddenly has not the thought
come, But what is it after all? What is anything that I have
ever done or ever can do? What is it to Him, the Lord of all the
world, and of a myriad, myriad worlds? "And who shall tell
my Lord" about this fragment of a thing?

"The Lord Himself, He Himself hears." There is no need
Psa. 139. 6   that any should tell Him, He Himself knows. "Such knowledge
Psa. 142. 3   is too wonderful for me". "When my spirit was overwhelmed
within me, then Thou knewest my path"; we can understand
that a little, but not this tender knowledge of the minute details
of common life—the oddments of life, tiny things we could
never gather up and look at and feel they were something, the
nothings of our day, those touches that do not show, but would
be missed if they were not there, and all the little songs of the
heart—"the Lord Himself, He Himself hears", sees, loves. Are
you not glad that David wrote that little Psalm?

[1] See Appendix, p. 193.

OCTOBER 28

Isa. 41. 8, 9 : LXX. *But thou . . . art My servant . . .*
whom I have chosen . . .
whom I have loved . . .
whom I have taken hold of from the ends
of the earth.
I have called thee . . .
I have chosen thee . . .
I have not forsaken thee . . .

These words have been a strength and a help to me. May they help some other servant of the great Master, child of the great Father, to-day. The devil is continually trying to discourage, but the loving Lord of all of us is continually encouraging. These are encouraging words.

OCTOBER 29

Rom. 5. 17 : *Shall reign in life by One, Jesus Christ.*

I was pondering over this (and it is an amazing word) when I noticed a verse on the same page—"He staggered not at the promise of God through unbelief; but was strong in faith, giving glory to God; and being fully persuaded that, what He had promised, He was able also to perform." I never connected these two great Scriptures before. But a light shone upon them this morning, so I pass it on. What a vision for the new day. We "shall reign in life"; "He is able . . . to perform." Let us not "stagger" at such promises. Rom. 4. 20, 21

OCTOBER 30

Mark 16. 3, 4 : *[The women] said among themselves, Who*
shall roll us away the stone from the door of the
sepulchre? And when they looked, they saw that
the stone was rolled away: for it was very great.
Matt. 28. 2 :   *And the angel of the Lord . . . came . . . and*
sat upon it.

Let us look out for the angels when impossible things lie ahead. Think of impossibilities being turned into seats for angels! Have we not a wonderful God? So whatever the difficulty is—something we do not know how to do, or some inward matter—we shall see it rolled away, and more than that, turned to some unexpected good. I do enjoy that calm word, And the angel sat upon it.

OCTOBER 31

Jude 25 : *To the only wise God our Saviour, be glory and majesty, dominion and power, both now and ever.*

"Both now and ever." "Ever" must really mean from this minute on, but we generally think of the words as meaning after time ends, and as I wrote the words "both now and ever", I thought how much easier it is to say "ever" than to say "now". It is easier to believe that the future will be full of the glory of the Lord, and His majesty, dominion and power, than to believe that to-day may be so—*this* day with its daily round and common task.

But our God does not want us to postpone to the future the joy of saying by our lives, "*Now* unto Him . . . be glory both *now* and ever."

NOVEMBER 1   ALL SAINTS' DAY

Heb. 11. 40 : *That they without us should not be made perfect.*

"They" are those who have walked the walk, run the race, fought the fight and passed out of sight. But with the passage that follows, which I understand to be an illustration taken from the arena with its surrounding tiers of watchers, it surely must mean this : we and they are still parts of one another, our victories delight them, fill up the measure of their perfection of joy, because they delight in Him Who is their sole delight. Let us give joy to the Heavenly host to-day. They are somewhere near enough to see us. Let us give joy to their Lord and ours by being as never before, all one in the love that passes knowledge. "Beloved, let us love".

NOVEMBER 2

Eph. 3. 15 : *The whole family in Heaven and earth*

Is it not glorious to belong to "the whole family"? And the word means one's own family; but notice how both Eph. 3. 14, 15 and Heb. 12. 1 direct us back to the highest of all—"I bow my knees unto the Father of our Lord Jesus Christ, of Whom the whole family in Heaven and earth is named" . . . "Wherefore, seeing we also are compassed about with so great a cloud of witnesses, . . . let us run . . . looking unto Jesus the Author and Finisher of our faith; Who for the joy that was set before Him endured the Cross, despising the shame, and is set down at the right hand of the throne of God."

So it is always. The joy of the family, invisible and visible, must fall back; we must press through it and find ourselves where, alone in the Presence of our God, we bow the knee to Him, and then go forth to run, looking at our Lord, crucified and risen again, "Who for the joy that was set before Him endured . . . "

NOVEMBER 3

2 Thess. 2. 1 : *Our gathering together unto Him.*

These words have been a continual comfort to me of late. We may be separated now, we may see little of some whom we want to see often. There are many partings in life; never once are we promised the joy of long continuance together here, but "our gathering together unto Him" is a certain joy. Every day as it passes brings us nearer that day when we shall gather together unto Him. If it can be such joy to be together here (and I at least have drunk deep of that joy), what will it be to be gathered There?

NOVEMBER 4

Psa. 38. 9 : *Lord, all my desire is before Thee.*

Only a simple word. This afternoon, words would not come when I tried to pray, and this troubled me; and then it was as if He, Who is never far away, said, What does it matter about words, when all thy desire is before Me? Perhaps you, too, find that words will not come when you wish they would. So I pass on my comfort.

In St Augustine's words : "To Him Who is everywhere, men come, not by travelling, but by loving."

It is not far to go for Thou art near,
It is not far to go for Thou art here;

And not by travelling, Lord, men come to Thee,
But by the way of love, and we love Thee.

NOVEMBER 5

Gather my thoughts, good Lord, they fitful roam
    Like children bent on foolish wandering,
    Or vanity of fruitless wayfaring—
O call them home.

See them, they drift like the wind-scattered foam;
　　Like wild sea-birds, they hither, thither fly,
　　And some sink low, and others soar too high—
O call them home.

Wherever, Lord, beneath the wide blue dome
　　They wander, in Thy patience find them there:
　　That undistracted I may go to prayer—
O call them home.

NOVEMBER 6

I have been noticing how in the Psalms every experience of distress turns to a straight look-up, and praise. I had not noticed till recently that the Psalm of the weaned child (Psalm 131) ends like that: "O Israel, hope in the Lord from this time forth and for evermore." And to-day I read Psalm 69, and there again I found the look-up that ends in praise. Kay translates *v.* 10, "I wept soul-tears", and that is just what it is like at times, when all we have done to help another soul seems to end in failure. Even so, "I will praise the name of God with a song, and will magnify Him with thanksgiving." *v.* 30

Surely this emphasis on praise in the Psalms is because to turn from discouraging things and look up with a song in one's heart is the only sure way of continuance. We sink down into what David calls mire, slime, deep waters, if we do not quickly *v.* 2 look up, and turning our back on the discouraging, set our faces again toward the sunrising.

Perhaps that is what *v.* 32 of that Psalm means, "Ye that seek after God, let your heart live." "Oh let your heart revive". (Kay.)

I found all this very reviving. It led straight to "They that wait upon the Lord shall renew their strength", and "Let them that love Him be as the sun when he goeth forth in his might." Judges 5. 31

R.V.

Isa. 40. 31

NOVEMBER 7

Dryness . . . Rain.

I want to give you a word which has often come to me after a time of prayer; may it be to you what it has been to me: "Thou, O God, didst send a plentiful rain, whereby Thou didst Psa. 68. 9

confirm Thine inheritance when it was weary." The LXX has, "O God, Thou wilt grant to Thine inheritance a gracious rain; for it was weary, but Thou didst refresh it."

After prayer of the kind that is a real traffic with Heaven, we may be tired, there may be a dryness like the dryness of the burnt-up earth before rain. Here are words which we may turn into a prayer: O God, send a plentiful rain; confirm Thine inheritance for it is weary; refresh it. Do we ever bring His own words to Him, and find that He turns away? Never.

Sometimes the dryness is different. It is not the natural dryness after effort which has achieved, it is the tiredness of failure. "I could not get there"—who does not know the baffled feeling that is the worst sort of weariness after distracted prayer? Even so, there is the plentiful rain, the gracious rain; rain not for the deserving, but just for the needy. Thank God for His Book of books. Is there a need it cannot meet, a dryness it cannot refresh? Not one. Come unto Me, and I will refresh you. "In a place of green grass, there has He made me dwell."

Matt. 11. 28
Psa. 23. 2 LXX

NOVEMBER 8

I think distractions in prayer are often because we have let ourselves wander too far from the things that matter most at common times, and so we have slipped into an easily interrupted, easily distracted, frame of mind. We need to live more at home. "In Him we live, and move, and have our being" means simply this: "God is our Home".

Acts 17. 28

> Home of our hearts, lest we forget
>   What our redemption meant to Thee,
> Let our most reverent thought be set
>   Upon Thy Calvary.

These words speak of something that I find I cannot drop out of my day without loss. I believe that a few minutes given daily to an earnest look at Calvary would do more to help our prayer than we imagine. "So shall the sayings of my mouth, and the meditation of my heart, be pleasing continually before Thee, O Lord my helper, and my Redeemer."

Psa.19. 14
LXX

NOVEMBER 9

> Father of spirits, this my sovereign plea
> I bring again, and yet again to Thee.
>
> Fulfil me now with love that I may know
> A daily inflow, daily overflow.
>
> For love, for love my Lord was crucified,
> With cords of love He bound me to His side.
>
> Pour through me now : I give myself to Thee,
> O Love, that led my Lord to Calvary.

NOVEMBER 10

1 Thess. 2. 7, 8 : R.V. *We were gentle in the midst of you, as when a nurse cherisheth her own children: even so, being affectionately desirous of you, we were well pleased to impart unto you, not the Gospel of God only, but also our own souls, because ye were become very dear to us.*

There we have it all. That is what the unhindered flow of the waters of love can make each one of us to be. May God increase ou desire for this blessed fulness till our hearts cry out for it, and cannot be satisfied with anything less.

NOVEMBER 11

Psa. 138. 3 : *In the day when I cried Thou answeredst me, and strengthenedst me with strength in my soul.*

That word has been my very life for many a year. The Revised Version says, "Thou didst encourage me with strength in my soul." It is always the spiritual that matters most, and so the assault on the spirit is always fiercer than on the body. If only the soul is encouraged with strength ("much strength" the Prayer Book has it), then we can hold on and conquer. If the least weakness creeps in there, the nerve of strength is cut, and we sink. David under trial was not delivered from it at once; the answer to his prayer was strength in his soul. In the inner

P.B.V.

life of the spirit, all of us need far more than any other thing
that first and greatest answer of peace. "When I called upon
Thee, Thou heardest me : and enduedst my soul with much
strength."

v. 8 P.B.V.

May the Lord keep us in the place where He can "make
good His lovingkindness" towards us, and keep us singing "in

v. 5

the ways of the Lord [whatever the outward] : for great is the
glory of the Lord."

NOVEMBER 12
Delayed answers to prayer.

Sometimes God's answer to our prayer is "Wait". I was
reminded of this to-day as I thought of the great commanded
prayer in Psalm 2. 8: "Ask of Me, and I shall give Thee . . .
the uttermost parts of the earth for Thy possession." Then
came the thought of the two "buts" of Heb. 2. 8, 9, and the
"are become" of Rev. 11. 15: "And the seventh angel sounded;
and there were great voices in Heaven, saying, The kingdoms
of this world *are become* the kingdoms of our Lord, and of His
Christ; and He shall reign for ever and ever." A long interval
lies between the prayer and what may be called the answer.
The two "buts" fill the interval. "*But* now we see not yet all
things put under Him. *But* we see Jesus . . . crowned with
glory and honour". We look across from the one "but" to
the other, and so the interval is filled with peace.

There may be for us, in our small measure, something akin
to the suffering of death which, for Him Whom we follow,
lay between the prayer and the promise of Psalm 2. 8, and
the calm glory of fulfilment of Rev. 11. 15. But who would
ask for anything else? If He waited, may not we? Is not
"Wait" an answer?

NOVEMBER 13
Col. 2. 1 : R.V. *I would have you know how greatly I strive
for you . . .*

With what do I strive in my prayers?

(a) With all that says to me, What is the use of *your*
praying? So many others, who know more of prayer than you
do, are praying, what difference does it make whether *you*

pray or not? Are you sure that your Lord is listening? Of
course He is listening to the other prayers, but yours are of such
small account; are you really sure He is "bending His ear" to
you?

(b) With all that suggests that we are asked to give too much
time to prayer. There is so much to do. Why set aside so much
time just to pray?

(c) With all that discourages me personally—perhaps the
remembrance of past sin, perhaps spiritual or physical tiredness; with anything and everything that keeps me back from
what occupied St Paul so often—vital prayer.

"Lord, teach us to pray".

NOVEMBER 14

What will help me most in this striving?

(a) The certain knowledge that our insignificance does not
matter at all, for we do not come to the Father in our own
name, but in the Name of His beloved Son. His ear is always
open to that Name. Of this we can be certain.

(b) The certain knowledge that the suggestion that prayer is
waste of time is Satan's lie; he is much more afraid of our
prayer than of our work. (This is proved by the immense difficulties we always find when we set ourselves to pray. They are
much greater than those we meet when we set ourselves to
work.)

(c) The application of God's sure promises to meet our need.
For example, "I have blotted out, as a thick cloud, thy trans- Isa. 44. 22
gressions, and as a cloud, thy sins" and kindred words meet all
distress about sin. "He giveth power to the faint; and to them Isa. 40. 29-31
that have no might He increaseth strength . . ." and "My 2 Cor. 12. 9, 10
grace is sufficient for thee . . ." meet everything that spiritual
or physical weariness can do to hinder. "I said not unto the Isa. 45. 19
seed of Jacob, Seek ye Me in vain" meets all other difficulties.
Our God says to us, "Seek ye My face", and the moment we Psa. 27. 8
say to Him, "Thy face, Lord, will I seek", His mighty energies
come to the rescue and we can strive according to His working, Col. 1. 29
which worketh in us mightily.

Greater, far greater, is He that is in us than he that is
against us. Let us count on the greatness of God.

NOVEMBER 15

But are we to go on striving to the end ?

No, there is a point to which we come, when, utterly trusting the promise of our Father, we rest our hearts upon Him. It is then we are given what St Paul calls "access with confidence". But do not forget that this access is by faith, not by feeling; faith in Him, our living Lord. He Who says Come unto Me, does not push us away when we come. As we go on, led by the Holy Spirit Who so kindly helps our infirmities, we find ourselves in 1 John 5. 14, 15, and lastly in Phil. 4. 6, 7. "And this is the confidence that we have in Him, that, if we ask anything according to His will, He heareth us : And if we know that He hear us, whatsoever we ask, we know that we have the petitions that we desired of Him." "Be careful for nothing; but in everything by prayer and supplication with thanksgiving let your requests be made known unto God. And the peace of God, which passeth all understanding, shall keep your hearts and minds through Christ Jesus." It is good to remember that immediate answer to prayer is not always something seen, but it is always inward peace.

And if the day end otherwise, and we feel discouraged? Then tell Him so, "Nothing ashamed of tears upon Thy feet".[1] "Lord, Thou knowest all things; Thou knowest that I love Thee."

But do not settle down into an attitude of "It will never be different." It will be different if only, in earnest, we "follow on to know the Lord".

John. 6. 37 (Tamil)
Rom. 8. 26

John. 21. 17

Hos. 6. 3

NOVEMBER 16

Dan. 10. 19 : *O man greatly beloved, fear not; peace be unto thee, be strong, yea, be strong. And when He had spoken unto me, I was strengthened.*

1 Kings 19. 8 : *And [Elijah] arose, and did eat and drink, and went in the strength of that meat forty days and forty nights.*

---

[1] *St Paul,* by Frederic W. H. Myers.

The strength of Heavenly food is proved by the strong life afterwards. The Bible is full of such illustrations of the ways of our Lord with His lovers. He draws them apart to Himself, sometimes quite alone, sometimes with fellow-lovers, and He meets them, feeds them, strengthens them. From that point, not craving for what, if it continued, would become a spiritual luxury, they go on like the sun (this is rather a glorious word) that "rejoiceth as a strong man to run a race." Psa. 19. 5, 6

NOVEMBER 17

Luke 22. 32 : *I have prayed for thee, that thy faith fail not.*

These words have helped me mightily of late, and chiefly because of that for which our Lord prayed. He did not pray that Peter should be delivered from the strain of life in a cruel Roman prison, or from a torturing death. But He did pray that, through all that lay ahead, his faith should not fail. It took me back to that wonderful prayer for deliverance *out of*, not *from*, the crisis of trial. "Now is My soul troubled; and what shall I John 12. 27, 28 say? Father, save Me from this hour : but for this cause came I unto this hour. Father, glorify Thy name. Then came there a voice from Heaven, saying, I have both glorified it, and will glorify it again." "Bring Me safely out of the conflict", not "keep Me from entering into it". Only One Who prayed that prayer for Himself could pray so for another.

So the words were searching as well as comforting. What do I, in my inmost heart, desire? Is it ease or relief from the undesired, the unexplained? Is it any mere earthly good? Then my prayers for others will not do much for them; a fountain cannot rise higher than its spring. Perhaps this is why our prayers are sometimes ineffectual.

But the thought swings back to comfort again. He ever liveth to make intercession for us. He will not pray weaker prayers, Heb. 7. 25 easier prayers, for us than He prayed for Himself and then for His disciple. He will enable us to live the life which makes the prayer of John 12. 27, 28 possible, and then He will lead us on to the place where we can pray as He prayed for His dear Peter.

NOVEMBER 18

Psa. 68. 13 : *Though ye have lien among the pots. . . .*

I think we sometimes feel as though we had. Perhaps we have been specially eager to press through and up into the clear air, and meet our Lord in the radiant, intimate way granted to others, and we do not seem to have been able to do so. The more we looked towards Him Whom our soul loveth, the more we saw His dazzling purity, the more we felt "among the pots", sooty; like him who "would not lift up so much as his eyes unto Heaven"; like him who said, "Woe is me! for I am undone . . . for mine eyes have seen the King, the Lord of Hosts."

Luke 18. 13
Isa. 6. 5

"*Though* ye have lien among the pots, yet shall ye be as the wings of a dove covered with silver, and her feathers with yellow gold." It is the sun striking down upon the bird that gives that look of silver and gold. I have never seen it, on our doves and paddy-birds flying across the sky, without wonder and comfort that passes words. There is nothing too good for His love to do. Love transforms the thing it loves. The look of love transforms. We have lain among the pots, we have not risen to our opportunities. "I am undone" seems somehow to describe our condition. And yet our Lord, our glorious Lord, comes with this word to us, holding it out, as it were, in His pierced hands: "*Yet* shall ye be as the wings of a dove covered with silver, and her feathers with yellow gold."

NOVEMBER 19

Job 41. 32 : (Delitzsch) *He lighteth up the path behind him.*

This was said of a crocodile; how much more true it should be of a Christian. Before us a path shining more and more, behind us a path lighted up; and that is life as God means it to be, and not something dull and ordinary.

What does this text taken out of its context say to us to-day? I think just this : let us light up the path as we go on; like a ship moving through the night let us leave a bright track behind. No little patch of darkness, no tired mood, must find room in that path. "They looked unto Him, and were radiant";

Psa. 34. 5
Am.R.V.

"we all, with unveiled face beholding [or reflecting] as in a glass the glory of the Lord, are [being] transformed from glory to glory, even as by the Spirit of the Lord." Such verses show how this life may be ours.
2 Cor. 3. 18 A.V. and R.V.

NOVEMBER 20

Psa. 48. 8 : *As we have heard, so have we seen in the city of the Lord of hosts, in the city of our God: God will establish it for ever.*

Perhaps we are sad because of what seems a lost battle. But "a lost battle is one which one believes lost". The battle is the Lord's, not ours. The words "as we have heard, so have we seen" have heartened me again and again to believe to see the goodness of the Lord, when all that was happening seemed to say, You shall *not* see.

We have heard of Thy victories, O Lord our Captain, we shall see them again. As we have heard, so shall we see. The day will come when we shall say, *As we have heard, so have we seen.*

NOVEMBER 21

Psa. 22. Title LXX. *Concerning the Morning Aid.*

The titles of the Psalms in the LXX give us many thoughts. When we think of Psalm 22, we think most of the darkness and suffering of Calvary. We know that it was in our Saviour's mind through those most awful hours; He quoted the first verse, He fulfilled all the verses. Even though there is a burst of triumphant joy in that psalm of pain, it is chiefly the pain that comes to mind when we think of it. But its title is not about pain, it is a word of beautiful joy : *Concerning the Morning Aid.* As I pondered this, my thoughts were led on to a familiar New Testament story : "It was now dark and Jesus was not come to them . . . They see Jesus walking on the sea". Looking back on that night the most vivid memory must have been, not the darkness or the weariness, not the great wind and the rough sea, but the blessed Morning Aid that came before the morning. John 6. 17, 19

So let us not make too much of the storm of the night. "The darkness hideth not from Thee;" "He saw them toiling in Psa. 139. 12
Mark 6. 48

EDGES OF HIS WAYS

rowing". The wind was contrary unto them then, perhaps it is contrary to us now. But just when things were hardest in that tiredest of all times (between 2 a.m. and 6 a.m.), just then, He came.

John 14. 18 / **Hos. 6. 3 French Version** — "I will not leave you comfortless: I will come to you", He said, and He does come. He always will come. "His coming is as certain as the morning". His Morning Aid comes before the morning. If we do not see Him coming, even so, He is on **Matt. 28. 20** His way to us. More truly, He is *with* us. "I am with you all the days, and all the day long." (Moule.)

NOVEMBER 22

Psa. 94. 19 : LXX. *Thy consolations have soothed my soul.*

This Psalm is about the wrong things that happen in the world. Everyone who thinks at all, sooner or later is distressed by these triumphant evils; and sometimes discouraged thoughts **Kay** come, "busy thoughts"—as one translation has it—"while my busy thoughts multiply within me, Thy consolations delight **LXX** my soul", "Thy consolations have soothed my soul."

Perhaps, for some other reason, to-day finds us troubled. Busy thoughts, puzzled thoughts, sad thoughts, disappointed thoughts, anxious, perplexing thoughts, these can come in flocks, in strong multitudes. But with them, in larger flocks and stronger multitudes, come the blessed comforts of God. These comforts will delight us if only we will give them room in our hearts; they will soothe us, too, till the sense of trouble **John 14. 18** passes quite away. It is yesterday's lovely word again: "I will not leave you comfortless: I will come to you."

NOVEMBER 23

Souls in Caves

Psa. 142. *A Psalm of David when he was in a cave.*

It was not his fault that he was there. It is generally our fault when we find ourselves in a cave. The soul that is constantly thinking of what it likes or does not like; what it wants to do, or does not want to do; where it wants to be, or does not want to be—that soul is in a cave. But even for those foolish souls who go of their own will into caves, there are words of release; *vv.* 5, 7 say, "I cried unto Thee, O Lord : . . . Bring my soul out of prison". Pray this prayer in sincerity, and the soul is out of its cave—out in the blue open-air again.

Sometimes we wait for something special to happen. Do not wait. Look up to Him Who is near : "I cried unto *Thee*, O Lord". And notice one thing more—"Bring my soul out of prison, [not that I may do what I like best to do, but] *that I may praise Thy Name*."

NOVEMBER 24

Psalm 18.

Let us pray for one another that we may not go into caves. Any one of us might do it at any moment, but for the grace of God. The heading of this Psalm says that it is the Song which David spoke to the Lord . . . when he was delivered from all his enemies—those enemies who had driven him into the cave.

There are many caves besides the cave of selfishness and self-love, of which we thought yesterday; but whatever our cave is, the moment we get out, the devil is sure to tell us we shall soon be back again, and so the second verse in the LXX is delightful : "The Lord is my firm support".

Is that not just what we want? We know our weakness, we have proved it many a time; but we need not fall, for "the Lord is our firm support". I have noticed that some of the happiest people are not by nature the strongest, but they are those who love the Lord their Strength with a confident, joyful love; and they are not constantly thinking of themselves and their weakness, nor do they ever dream of *not* enjoying what He gives them to do, for "the joy of the Lord is [their] strength", and their Lord is their firm support. Neh. 8. 10

NOVEMBER 25

Rom. 15. 13 : *Now the God of hope fill you with all joy and peace in believing, that ye may abound in hope, through the power of the Holy Ghost.*

These golden words have been much in my heart. They do not open their strength and sweetness to any except to the seeker of souls. To such a one, especially in hours when it seems

as though all that has been done is as water spilt on the
ground—travail in vain, prayer in vain—these great words are
life and light. They are rock under foot. They are a stronghold
in the day of trouble.

I have been reading a book which deals with Rome about
the time when Paul wrote. The Jewish quarter, where probably
most of those lived who read these words of hope for the first
time, was a rabbit-warren of a place. The influences round the
Christians there were wholly weakening, demoralising and evil.
There must have been many a sad hour for any who were keen
to help others Heavenward. But no, they must not be sad.
What so often seems the losing side is the winning side. "Let

**Rom. 12. 12
Way**

your hope be something exultant," Paul writes, but how can
it be? It seems dried up at times. It is *then* that these words are

Ch. 15. 13 Way

spirit and life. The God of hope fill you . . . "so that this hope of
yours may be an overflowing fountain". We cannot fill ourselves
with hope; we have no wells of hope within us. But God has;
just as He is the God of Love, so that we can pray, Love
through me, Love of God : so He is the God of Hope, and we
may pray, *Hope through me*, Hope of God—yes, even for this
soul, for whom I have all but lost hope.

> Hope through me, God of Hope,
>   Or never can I know
> Deep wells and living streams of hope,
>   And pools of overflow.
>
> Flood me with hope to-day
>   For souls perverse, undone,
> For sinful souls that turn away,
>   Blind sunflowers, from their Sun.
>
> O blessed Hope of God,
>   Flow through me patiently,
> Until I hope for everyone
>   As Thou hast hoped for me.

NOVEMBER 26

We have all read St Paul's letters to his dear Timothy, and

**2 Tim. 1. 7
R.V.**

we all know that strong word about the "Spirit of . . . power
and love and discipline." Paul tells Timothy to be "mindful

again" that he has truly received that Spirit, and *not* the spirit of fear. (Perhaps Timothy was a good deal tempted to be afraid.) "I put thee in remembrance"—to be "mindful again".

God knows what we are most likely to forget, and He will remind us again of just that thing. Some may be finding themselves fearing lest they will not be able to go on to the end living that life which they know is the only life worth living. The Spirit of the Living God is not like a single gift put into the hands of a child. One of His symbols is water. As the water from the heights flows into the pool in the forest, not in the great rush of the monsoon time only, but every moment all the year round, causing a continual overflow, *so the blessed Spirit flows into our hearts*—needy (He knows how needy), empty, but for Him. He is not the Spirit of fear, "but of power and love and discipline."

NOVEMBER 27

2 Tim. 1. 7 : *The Spirit of Power.*

How long does it take the grace of God to run from Him to us? How long does it take the current of electricity to run from the Power-house to any room which is connected with it? It is most heartening to think of the wonderful speed with which the help we need is sent to us. Less than half a minute, less than half a second, is enough to make us strong in the strength of our God. "God hath not given us the spirit of fear; but of power . . ."

One day I was in trouble and oppressed about many things. It was one of those days when everything seems to go wrong. I was trying to get my Quiet Time but was constantly interrupted. Suddenly these words came—I could hardly believe they were in the Bible, they seemed so new to my needy heart—"Grace to help in time of need." I found them and read them and marked them with joy, and in that moment, the moment of their coming, I was renewed in strength.

Heb. 4. 16

Are you in special need to-day? Blessed be the Spirit of Power—blessed be the speed with which He flies to our relief. This is my word from Him to you : "Let us come boldly unto the throne of grace, that we may obtain mercy, and find *grace to help in time of need.*"

NOVEMBER 28

2 Tim. 1. 7 : *The Spirit of Love.*

In Tamil we have a polite word, which tells someone who asks for something, that we have nothing to give; we have run short of it— *Poochiam.*

One day, I felt like saying *Poochiam* about love, I had run short of it. I was in the Forest, and I had just read a letter which was hard to answer lovingly. I was sitting by The Pool at the time, and presently began to watch the water flow down through the deep channel worn in the smooth rocks above it. There was always inflow, so there was always outflow. Never for one minute did the water cease to flow in, and so never for one moment did it cease to flow out; and I knew, of course, that the water that flowed out was the water that flowed in. The hollow that we call The Pool had no water of its own, and yet all the year round there was an overflow.

"God hath not given you the Spirit of fear, . . . but of love". If love flows in, love will flow out. Let love flow in. That was the word of the pool. There is no need for any of us to run short of love. We need never say *Poochiam.*

NOVEMBER 29

2 Tim. 1. 7 : R.V. : *The Spirit of Discipline.*

"And of Discipline." This word has become precious to many of us. Some of us have read a book called by this name,[1] and found much strong food there; and all of us who are in earnest to press on and follow our Lord, know that we must learn to welcome the Spirit of discipline, just as truly as we welcome the Spirit of power and of love.

It is the Spirit of discipline we need when the *I* in us rises and says, I want this, I want that; this work is to my liking, that work is not. We get nowhere till we welcome the brave Spirit Who never hesitates to ask us to do hard things; Who never fails to strengthen us to do them; Who can even make us eager to do them, choosing the strenuous rather than the easy,

---

[1] *The Spirit of Discipline,* by Francis Paget, Bp of Oxford.

the climb uphill rather than the level. Over and over again these words come to my heart : *All Christ's life was a cross and a martyrdom; and thou seekest to thyself rest and joy?* (Thomas à Kempis.)

NOVEMBER 30

2 Tim. 1. 12 : *For I know Whom I have believed, and am persuaded that He is able to keep that which I have committed unto Him against that day.*

When St Paul wrote to Timothy, "I know Whom I have believed," soon after speaking of the Spirit of power and love and discipline, he was thinking of his own matters, but his words come to us with very great comfort. We think of our souls which the Lord has redeemed, we know their weakness— up one day, down the next; unstable, not to be counted on at all—how can we possibly be sure we shall not stumble on the road before the end of the journey? But "I know Whom I have believed, and am persuaded that He is able to keep that which I have committed unto Him against that day."

Psa. 138. 8 is a beautiful prayer in Tamil, "Let not slip [as a ring from a finger] the works of Thine own hands."

So we need not fear : God hath not given us the spirit of fear. As we turn from that spirit and refuse him room in our hearts, the Lord Whom we know ("I know Whom I have believed") will draw us so close to Himself that we shall be persuaded that He will indeed keep us, on to the end.

DECEMBER 1

2 Esdras 1. 30

The book of Esdras was written in B.C. 623. In it are these words, "As a hen gathereth her chickens under her wings". I wonder if our Lord Jesus was quoting from that book (just as He often quoted from books in the Old Testament) when He grieved over the city of Jerusalem. Books that we know He read, or think He may have read, are always specially interesting to read. We feel as though we were reading with Him, and come very close to Him; so I think you will find something in the following words from this old book. The prophet is speaking of a building which he saw in a vision, and he says, "Fear not,

2 Esdras
10. 55, 56

let not thine heart be affrighted, but go thy way in, and see the beauty and greatness of the building, as much as thine eyes be able to see : and then shalt thou hear as much as thine ears may comprehend."

Every morning each one of us enters into a new day. "Fear not, . . . but go thy way in" (He Whom thou lovest goeth before), and then look. There is much to see—things that tell of His love and grace; things that show His Presence; the treasures of His Book. There is no limit to what we shall see except the limit of our power to see. "Open Thou mine eyes" is a prayer for us all.

And then listen. There is much to hear. What did God say to me this morning in what I read in His Book, in what I heard from others who love Him, in what I heard deep in my heart, through something He caused me to recall? Whatever it was, let me take time to "comprehend" it, hold it fast, and live in the light of it to-day.

DECEMBER 2

Ezek. 1. 25 : *There was a voice from the firmament that was over their heads, when they stood, and had let down their wings.*

One night I was much troubled by anxious thoughts; they came beating on me through those hours, and I could not get

away from them; I could hear no reassuring voice. At last I
remembered Ezekiel 1, which I had read the day before, and
I began to see that the wings of the will and the wings of the
work were not the only wings that must be let down, there were
others, there were the wings of anxious thoughts.

Those wings were not easy to let down, but when at last
they were down, this was the word: "Hast thou not known? Isa. 40. 28, 29
hast thou not heard, that the everlasting God, the Lord, the
Creator of the ends of the earth, fainteth not, neither is weary?
. . . He giveth power to the faint; and to them that have no
might He increaseth strength."

Do you not think that the wings of anxious thoughts are
sometimes the hardest of all to let down? But we have a tender
Father. He can reassure us about those whom we love so much
and for whom we are tempted to be anxious. He will be for
them "a refuge from the storm, a shadow from the heat, when   Isa. 25. 4
the blast of the terrible ones is as a storm against the wall."

This was the word of the Voice from the firmament, when at
last I was helped to let down those weary wings of anxious
thoughts which had troubled me.

DECEMBER 3

Psa. 18. 9-11 : *Darkness was under His feet . . . His pavilion
round about Him were dark waters and thick
clouds of the skies.*

I found great comfort one day in these verses. It was when
God was flying upon the wings of the wind to the relief of His
servant, that His servant, looking up, saw thick clouds of the
skies. The pavilion of the Lord is not always a golden glory,
such as our sunrises so often open before us. It is sometimes
darkness. He made darkness His secret place; His pavilion
round about Him dark waters, thick clouds of the skies.

You will wonder where the comfort came in. Quite simply :
long ago we chose Mary's favourite place—"Mary . . . sat at   Luke 10. 39
Jesus' feet, and heard His word." If we, who would always
abide there, find ourselves at any time wrapped in darkness, it
is only because we are in the cloud that is under His feet, for it
is written, "darkness was under His feet", and "the clouds are   Psa. 18. 9
the dust of His feet."   Nahum 1. 3

DECEMBER 4

Several evenings lately we have seen something very beautiful. It was, as it were, a sunset in the east. To the west there was not the faintest hint of colour. The mountains were dark against a dark sky. Heavy clouds, indigo blue and grey, lay over the forest. There was no light in the west, and yet the eastern sky was aglow. The plains lay like a jewelled carpet, and the sky was golden and then a soft rose-pink. That sky saw what we could not see. It saw the light of the sun that was shining beyond the clouds that closed our valley in and covered our mountains. It was looking at and reflecting that great glory.

Was it not a lovely parable?

DECEMBER 5

I have been helped very much by some of the "Evens" that the Revised Version brings to light. You know how sometimes words take life for us. It is as if they were made known to us in an altogether new way, and we are conscious of the Touch of God. I think Proverbs 22. 19 R.V. explains that : "*I* have made them [those words] known to thee this day, *even to thee*." So every such experience is a definite act of the Lord, even to me.

Then in chapter 23. 15 there is a lovely "Even". It is all of Him if we are made aware of His Presence and listen when He speaks, and so receive wisdom; but in His extraordinary love He speaks as if it were all our doing, "If thine heart be wise, My heart shall be glad, *even* Mine." Is that not an amazing word? Think of such as we being allowed to add to the gladness of God. It is an overwhelming thought.

And then there is the dear "Even mine" of 2 Sam. 22. 2 R.V. "The Lord is my Rock, and my Fortress, and my Deliverer, *even mine*". The comfort of that comes again and again.

DECEMBER 6

Matt. 14.20; Mark 6. 43; Luke 9. 17; John 6. 12; (all R.V.)
Broken pieces

Have you ever felt at the end of the day that you had nothing to offer but "broken pieces" of things? In the morning we put our day in our Lord's hands. Then we began to do His work, but we were not able to do nearly as much as we had hoped. Interruptions came and broke up our plans, and the evening finds us a little disappointed. "I hoped to do so much, and I have done nothing worth bringing to Thee"—that is how we feel. I have been finding new comfort in the two words, which are used by each of the four evangelists in telling the end of the story of the feeding of the Five Thousand. They speak of "broken pieces", and the same words are used by two in telling of the later miracle. There was nothing over but broken pieces, and yet of those fragments our Lord said, Gather them up that nothing be lost. Even so, our dear Lord cares for the broken pieces of our lives, the fragments of all we meant to do, the little that we have to gather up and offer, and He will use even these fragments. He will not let even the least of our little broken things be lost. Matt. 15. 37 & Mark 8. 8

DECEMBER 7

Psa. 36. 8, 9 :
R.V.
and P.B.V.

They shall be abundantly satisfied with the plenteousness of Thy house: and Thou shalt make them drink of the river of Thy pleasures. For with Thee is the fountain of life.

This is a glorious word for to-day. There is not a dull day in life as God means it to be, nor a starved and thirsty day, for "the river of God is full of water", and the natural thing is to be happy—the unnatural is to be depressed. Psa. 65. 10 P.B.V.

And yet we all know that a curious sort of dullness can creep over the soul at times, and I have been finding all sorts of help in Psa. 30. 11, which seems to have been written for such occasions, and probably was. "Thou hast turned my heaviness into joy :" "Thou hast *torn off* my sackcloth and girded me with gladness." Could anything possibly be more delightful and more vigorous? I do like the "torn off". v. 12 P.B.V. & Rotherham

So if any of us feel that scratchy sense of sackcloth on the inner man that makes for heaviness, let us change the tense, as we always may, and fastening our eyes on the Lord our Strength say, Lord, tear off my sackcloth, gird me with gladness, to the end that I—yea even I—"may sing praise to Thee, and not be silent."

"Abundantly satisfied with the plenteousness of Thy house",
made to "drink of the river of Thy pleasures", "girded with
gladness"; how can we be silent?

DECEMBER 8

Job 34. 29 : *When He giveth quietness, who then can make
trouble ?*

I wonder if poor Job, who was weary of words that darkened
knowledge, felt like answering, Nobody, not even you. It would
have been the true answer. Not all the Elihus in the world can
make trouble when God gives quietness. What is my "Elihu"
at the moment? Most of us have one or two. Some have a good
many. They can do us no harm, they cannot spoil that inner
quietness which must be if God's perfect peace is to be ours.
But supposing they do somehow succeed in disturbing us, and
we suddenl find ourselves ruffled just when we most wanted to
be peaceful; then there is one certain and swift way back into
peace : one upward look—Thy pardon, Lord; Thy stillness,
Lord—and that which went from us returns. We have peace
from the God of peace.

DECEMBER 9

Song of Songs 4. 8 : *Look from the top.*

This is a splendid word for a busy day with its crush of work
of all sorts. If we get caught in the crush and pushed down, so
to speak, the next thing we know is that we are grovelling in the
dust. Things are on the top of *us*, we are not on the top of
anything. So the word comes, "Look from the top". Come with
Me from all that, come up the mountain with Me, "look from
the top". In every-day life this simply means, look from everything up to the Lord Jesus, Who is our Peace, our Victory and
our Joy, for we *are* where we *look*. From below, things feel
impossible, people seem impossible (some people at least), and
we ourselves feel most impossible of all. From the top we see as
our Lord sees; He sees not what *is* only, but what shall be. He
is not discouraged, and as we look with Him, our discouragement vanishes, and we can sing a new song.

> But when from mountain top,
>   My Lord, I look with Thee,
> My cares and burdens drop
>   Like pebbles in the sea.
>   The air is clear,
>   I fear no fear,
>   In this far view
>   All things are new.

DECEMBER 10

Rom. 5. 17 : *Much more they which receive abundance of grace . . . shall reign in life by One, Jesus Christ.*

There is a lovely word in this verse, it is "abundance". The word is translated "overflowing" in Weymouth and elsewhere, and Way has "The measureless overflowing of the fountain of the grace of God". This is the grace that is ready to help us in time of need, this and nothing less. Thank God, He does not measure out grace in teaspoons. The measureless overflowings of the fountain are for each one of us to-day. Need we fail? NEVER.

DECEMBER 11

Heb. 10. 22-24 : *Let us . . . Let us . . . Let us . . .*

Let us draw near. This word shines out in my reading to-day. "It is good for me to draw near to God;" "As for me, nearness to God is my good;" "The drawing near of God is blessedness." It is as though the different translations were trying to find words joyful enough and eager enough to tell this that human words can never tell. "To draw nigh to Him, and abide with Him, must be man's highest good", is Kay's lovely note. Are we in earnest to draw near, or are we contenting ourselves by thinking, or singing, or even praying, about it? We shall never draw near until we fling every hindering thing to the winds, and get up and do so.

Let us hold fast. This word, too, implies a vigorous action. If we relax, things slip. If, having drawn near as we believed, we are satisfied with that and live on our past experiences, we shall

(margin note: Psa. 73. 28, Kay Roth.)

find they are like the sand which a child gathers up and seems
to hold, but which has slipped between his fingers before he
knows it. To *lay hold* in the sense of Heb. 10. 23 asks for a
gathering up of the energies of the soul.

Let us consider one another. Are we out to help one another
Heavenward, or just to get to Heaven ourselves? The different
translations are very searching: "Let us withal keep watch
over each other, to stimulate each other to love and noble
deeds." "Let us attentively consider one another to provoke
unto love and noble works." "Let us bestow thought on one
another with a view to arousing one another to brotherly love
and right conduct." Notice how love comes first every time, for
it includes all.

There is something that is altogether unearthly for each of us
in what is given when in truth we *draw near,* either alone (this
must come first), or with others like-minded. Then there must
be the strong *holding fast,* something that will not give way
under stress, or loneliness, or disappointment, or any other
thing. And there must be *help to others* as opportunity is given.

DECEMBER 12

Psa. 25. 10: *All the paths of the Lord are mercy and truth.*

All, not some; not only those we would naturally choose; but
all. This was my word this morning. And mercy means lovingkindness. "All the paths of the Lord are loving-kindness". Is
not this a beautiful word and a Heavenly? There is a path
which each of us must walk quite alone. We may be one of a
family, even so we walk that path alone. The dearest of our
dear ones cannot walk there with us. "He who follows Him the
nearest needs must walk alone."

Yet we are not alone for a single moment in that path which
is one long stretch of loving-kindness and leads straight to the
City of Light, the Vision of His Face. Though we do not see
Him now, yet He companions us; and, as we look back, we see
that the path was always mercy and truth, and we know it is
just the same to-day, and it will be the same to the end. Let us
rest our hearts on this very lovely word: "All the paths of the
Lord are mercy and truth", lovingkindness and truth.

Way.

Roth.
Weym.

R.V.

DECEMBER 13

2 Cor. 2. 14 : *Now thanks be unto God, Which always causeth us to triumph in Christ.*

There is not the faintest expectation of defeat here, so when we say or feel that we cannot help giving way, we are going straight against the expectation of the Spirit.

Sometimes when we read about victory and peace and so on, we find ourselves wondering what the writer has been through. Is he writing from his armchair or from the thick of battle? When we read these amazing words we have no such question. I have been thinking of one item in the list given in Ch. 11 of this letter, the eight floggings. Apart from the clamour and misery and injustice, there was severe pain. *One* such experience would be enough for a life-time, so we should feel. St Paul had eight. It makes one feel ashamed of ever making much of anything. But this is the one who could write, "Thanks be to God Which *always* causeth us to triumph in Christ".

DECEMBER 14

Phil. 1. 10, 11 : *That ye may be sincere, and without offence . . . being filled with the fruit of righteousness.*

This is a prayer that goes deep into the heart of things— "fruit which is borne through Jesus Christ . . . to God's praise and glory." (Moule.) We know what the lovely fruit is : love, joy, peace, longsuffering, gentleness, goodness, faith, meekness, self-control (see R.V. margin)—that power which can say, as our Lord did, *I must*, that "spirit of discipline" which carries the *I must* into effect. With that word I always put this, "God hath not given us the spirit of fear; but of power, and of love, and of discipline."

Gal. 5. 22-23

2 Tim. 1. 7
A.V. & R.V.

Truth at the root, sincerity which is clearness (Bishop Moule gives this as the meaning of the word), the life of our Lord rising through us like sap through the branch of a tree, and the fruit, something that will be to the praise and glory of God. It sounds too much to believe possible for such as we are, so is it not a comfort that all this is in a prayer?

DECEMBER 15

Col. 3. 12 : (Way) *Array yourselves, then, as God's chosen ones, His consecrated and dearly loved ones, in a heart of sympathy, in kindness, in lowliness, in gentleness, in tireless patience.*

v. 5 That is the end of all true "doing to death"—the end is life, not death; a life of uttermost love, love that cannot help loving any more than the sun can help shining, or the river flowing, or the trees putting forth green leaves.

The bond that holds God's children together is love, just love. One unkind deed, one unkind word, one *thought* even that moves towards unkindness, is fatal to the quality of love we must have if His love is to be in us. It is not a little thing to love like this. Lord, evermore give us this love.

DECEMBER 16

Eph. 4. 2, 3 : *Forbearing one another in love; endeavouring to keep the unity of the Spirit in the bond of peace.*

This word has been much in my heart. The different translations bring out the thought of the need of effort; this kind of
Weym. living does not come of itself—"Bearing with one another lovingly [there will always be something that needs to be lovingly borne with], and earnestly striving to maintain, in the
Way. uniting bond of peace, the unity given by the Spirit." "Show to one another the patience of love [there will always be need of patience]. Be earnest to maintain the unity of which the Spirit is the Author, linked together by the chain of God's peace."

These words do not suggest that we shall easily guard this precious thing, the vital unity of love. But if we are in earnest about it, there is nothing to fear; for this, and nothing less, is the will of God concerning us.

DECEMBER 17

Burning still

"She hath neither rusted out, nor burned out. She is burning still." I read that in an Australian magazine and I prayed that it might be true of each one of us. We want most earnestly not to rust out, we would gladly be burned out, but till that day comes, the Lord keep us "burning still."

Perhaps some of us are sorely tempted to think that just now there is not much that is "burning" about our lives. Some are ill, some have duties of a very simple sort—where does the burning come in? Where did it come in when John the Baptist was shut up in prison? He could not do anything but just endure, and not be offended, and not doubt his Lord's love. But when our Lord Jesus spoke of him, He said he was burning and shining—"a burning and a shining light".

John 5. 35

It is not the place where we are, or the work that we do or cannot do, that matters, it is something else. It is the fire within that burns and shines, whatever be our circumstances.

DECEMBER 18

Luke 7. 22, 23 : *Go your way, and tell John . . .*

Before they got to the end of the mighty things they were to tell him, his heart must have kindled with new hope : My Lord can do all that, He is doing all that, He is omnipotent. He is my loving Lord, and He is very near. He Who is doing all these things will do great things for me. I shall soon be free—He Who is opening the prison doors of death will open my prison door. Can you not all but hear him say it, or at least feel him think it, as he listens to the story of "what things" these men of his "have seen and heard"? And then, instead of a promise, and quick help, "Blessed is he, whosoever shall not be offended in Me", and that was all. But it was enough. John accepted the unexplained. And a light shone in the cell, and in that light he lived till his prison door opened, and he stepped across its threshold into the Land of Light.

Matt. 11. 6

To many of you this is a familiar word, but it came to me afresh as I read these two verses one after the other last night, and it spoke to me as I thought of the many who are being trusted not to be offended in Him.

DECEMBER 19

Psa. 103. 20 : *Bless the Lord, ye His angels, that excel in strength, that do His commandments, hearkening unto the voice of His word.*

"Not only mightily executing the word, when heard; but ever intently listening, *ready to catch the intimation of His*

Will" is Kay's note. "Ever intently listening," as though to emphasize the new listening for each new word; for there is nothing stale in the life to which we are called. Ruts are of the devil. We must have fresh manna every day—yesterday's will not do. Our Lord's whole life is an illustration of what it means to live with an ear sensitive to the lightest indication of the wish of the Father. (For example, see John 7. 6-10.) So that where obedience to His commands is in question, just as much as where it is a matter of our own heart's nourishment, the hearing heart is the first of our needs.

I have been thinking, too, of how this thought is bound up with, or lies behind, the great prayer promises. For how can we "know" in the sense of 1 John 5. 14, 15, if we have not given time to listen to our Father's thought about the petition we bring Him? and it is set deep in our Lord's words about the difference between servants and friends.

John 15. 15

But the gold in this mine is inexhaustible. May the Lord of all spiritual riches lead us deeper in. We shall find ourselves low at His feet: "I am but a little child: I know not how to go out or come in . . . Give therefore thy servant a hearing heart".

1 Kings 3. 7, 9
mar.

DECEMBER 20

Book of Baruch 3. 34 : (B.C. 200.) *The stars shined in their watches, and rejoiced; when He calleth them, they say, Here we be; and so with cheerfulness they shewed light unto Him that made them*—or as the R.V. says, *They shined with gladness unto Him* ch. 6. 60 *that made them . . . For sun, moon, and stars being bright, and sent to do their offices, are obedient.*

Some of us have learned great things from the stars; and we can understand these words, they speak to us all. Are we "shining with gladness" to Him Who made us? If we are not in the place we would have chosen, do we shine with gladness *there*, or do we grumble inwardly, if not outwardly, and wish things were different? God make us all obedient like His sun and moon and stars, and help us to shine gladly to Him Who made us.

DECEMBER 21

Sometimes when we fail and have to ask for forgiveness, we are terribly tempted to weakness. We have failed so often, shall we ever be "more than conquerors"? Yesterday I read this: Rom. 8. 37
"He hath anointed me . . . to strengthen with forgiveness those Luke 4. 18
that are bruised". So to be forgiven is to be strengthened. We need not weaken, even in hope, if He Who forgives us strengthens us with forgiveness. The words are from the Aramaic Gospel, the very oldest (so some believe) of all the written Gospels. Therefore, the words may be indeed the very words our Lord Jesus spoke, or the first meaning of the words He spoke, for He spoke in Aramaic. Are they not beautiful and comforting?

DECEMBER 22

These days are full of thoughts of Him "Who for the joy Heb. 12. 2
that was set before Him endured". To the children, the manger is the chief thought, to us who are older (though we are children together at Christmas-time) the Cross always stands near the manger. It is the background to every picture, invisible, but there.

In a book on early French life in Canada I found a heroic story. It is that of a French missionary to the Indians of the dense forests of Huron, who, inspired by the life of another, made a "vow of perpetual stability", which meant the giving of his whole life to those to whom he had been sent. In speaking of this to one who found it hard to understand, he said—and the words are unforgettable—"Listen, my friend, no man can give himself heart and soul to one thing, while in the back of his mind he cherishes a desire, a secret hope, for something very different. You know that even in worldly affairs nothing worthwhile is accomplished except by that last sacrifice, the giving of oneself altogether and finally."

> Christ my Master beckoneth,
> Christ my Lord, the Crucified;
> He thus callèd reckoneth
> All the world as nought beside.
> Show me not imagined loss:
> I see His Cross.

DECEMBER 23

John 17. 26 : *That the love wherewith Thou hast loved Me
        may be in them.*

O Father, help, lest our poor love refuse
For our beloved the life that they would choose,
And in our fear of loss for them, or pain,
        Forget eternal gain.

Teach us to pray; O Thou Who didst not spare
Thine Own Belovèd, lead us on in prayer;
Purge from the earthly, give us love Divine,
        Father, like Thine, like Thine.

Last night, as I read in St John, I felt the force of our Lord's
prayer that the love wherewith His Father loved Him may be
in us. The most I had ever prayed had been for love that did
not refuse the uttermost for one I loved. "O Father, help, lest
our poor love refuse" puts that prayer into words, and I have
often found it difficult to reach even that. This prayer of our
Lord for us reaches infinitely further, for the love wherewith
the Father loved Him was the love that caused Him to *give*
that beloved One to suffering for the salvation of a lost world.
This is very different from, and far surpasses, the love that only
does not refuse that a beloved one shall suffer.

Christmas-time is full of thoughts of the Father's giving;
this thought will deepen all our thinking about it. What do we
know of such love? What do I know of it? Am I prepared to
give one whom I love to pain or to loss, as the Father gave, if
only others may be blessed? This, nothing less, was what the
love wherewith the Father loved the Son caused Him to do. It
was this love and no other that our Lord prayed should be in
us. Is it not a searching thought, a searching prayer?

DECEMBER 24   CHRISTMAS EVE

In this season of much singing I ask those who love our Lord
Jesus to ask very specially for singing hearts. It would be sad
if the lovely Christmas hymns and carols sounded only like a
noise—even a noise of music—to Him. But if they are the glad
and wondering adoration of our hearts, then I think they will

give Him joy. Do not forget what Christmas cost Him—
Gethsemane and Calvary.

DECEMBER 25   CHRISTMAS DAY

Once a star rose in the sky,
Silver star of mystery,
But the wise men pondering knew
What it said that they must do.

So in that first Christmas-tide
On their camels they did ride,
Rode to far Jerusalem,
Rode to farther Bethlehem;

Found the little precious Child,
On the ground before Him piled
Gold and frankincense and myrrh,
Hailed Him Royal Conqueror.

Once again, led by a Star
Do we come from near and far,
Drawn by Love's belovèd cords,
Hail our Saviour, Lord of lords.

And as holy Seraphim
Veil their faces, worship Him,
Pray we now this Christmas grace,
Reverence as we seek His Face.

DECEMBER 26

When I was small, I used to feel a kind of flat feeling after
Christmas Day was over, Now it has gone, and it will not come
again for a whole year. Sometimes we are in a curious way cast
down after something smaller, but much looked-forward to, is
over, some pleasure, something we do not want to think of as
past, and yet it has passed. God knows all about that feeling,
and there is a lovely verse for the comfort He has for it. It is
"God, that comforteth those that are cast down, comforted us
by the coming [the presence] of Titus." Often and often the
coming, the presence, of someone we love has comforted us

2 Cor. 7. 6 &
R.V. mar.

John 14. 18

Lam. 3. 23
Matt. 28. 20
when we were cast down—we all know that. And the Dearest of all dear friends is always coming to us in such moments, "I will not leave you comfortless: I will come to you." His Presence is like His compassions, "new every morning", yet perpetual. "Lo, I am with you alway [all the days, and all the da; long], even unto the end of the world."

DECEMBER 27

Phil. 2. 1 : (Way) *By all the encouragement you find in Messiah's nearness . . .*

Dr Way thinks that Paul's "hired house" was probably a room in a crowded lodging-house. It is not likely that he could have afforded more. He was of course chained to a soldier; the four walls of his room made his prison. It is worth-while to give oneself time to realise such circumstances. There must have been noise, crowding, loneliness, no privacy, not much outlook, little if any beauty, and, above all, a terrific temptation to feel as though he were not getting on with things. There was unsaved Rome all round and a tremendous drain on courage. Is it not as true to-day, as ever it was, that the golden secret of courage is found in the ungrieved presence of our Lord? "All the encouragement you find in Messiah's nearness".

DECEMBER 28

Phil. 2. 1 : (Way) *By all love's comforting power.*

Ch. 2. 19, 20
Ch. 1. 18 Moffat

Ch. 1. 9, 10
There are two simple illustrations of love in this letter that have been helping me. Love knows how to do without what it naturally wants. Love knows how to say, "What does it matter?"

"And it is my prayer that your love may be more and more rich in knowledge and in all manner of insight, enabling you to have a sense of what is vital". A moment later he has to refer to something trying to the spirit, but Love which enables to "a sense of what is vital" comes to the rescue at once. He does not brood over it or worry, for "what does it matter?"

"Some indeed 'actually for envy and strife . . . are proclaiming the Christ . . . from motives of faction . . . thinking to raise up tribulation for me in my bonds. Shall I give way to the trial and lose patience and peace? . . . Nay; what matters it? Is not the fiery arrow quenched in Christ for me?" (Moule.) It will not touch the glory of God, the ultimate victory of truth. Love accepts the trying things of life without asking for explanations. It trusts and is at rest. "Love's comforting power." Lord, evermore give us this love.

DECEMBER 29

Rev. 17. 14 : R.V. *These shall war against the Lamb, and the Lamb shall overcome them, for He is Lord of lords, and King of kings; and they also shall overcome that are with Him.*

These last nine words have been truly spirit and life to me. Sometimes it seems as if the war were against *us*, but it never is. It is against the Lamb, and the Lamb shall overcome. It is impossible to imagine anything else but victory for "the Lamb slain from the foundation of the world." So all that matters is that we should be with Him, "called and chosen and faithful."

Ch. 13. 8

> O God of peace, strong is the enemy,
>   But Thou art nigh;
> And he must fall beneath our feet,
>   Because of Calvary.

DECEMBER 30

Isa. 14. 31 : R.V. margin : *There is no straggler in his ranks.*

There are no stragglers in the ranks of the enemy. There must not be any in ours. As the year draws to a close, let us the more earnestly see to it that none of us is a straggler in spirit, drawing back from the hardest things, shirking what it means to fight the good fight of faith.

I suppose none of us is beyond the temptation to weaken, to "straggle". It goes on to the end. But with us is the Lord of Hosts, and He has strength enough and to spare for the weakest

and least soldierly of us all. So we need not "straggle", and by
Eph. 6. 10 His grace we will begin the New Year "strong in the Lord, and
in the power of His might."

DECEMBER 31

Two lines of a Keswick hymn are always with me as the year
closes :

> The Cross now covers my sin,
> The past is under the Blood.

Nothing can ever make these words of none effect. They are
mighty to comfort the soul and to set it on its way humble and
yet strong.

Looking back there is so much to grieve over. We can see
nothing at all in ourselves to praise, but so much in our Saviour.
His patience has never failed. He has never given up hope for
us. There is something very heartening in this. All that we see
See Psa. 139. 16 as sin, He sees, He saw, and far, far more. But "Thou knewest
me before I was", so nothing in me can surprise Him out of
loving me, there is wonderful comfort in that. The Cross
covers, the Blood cleanses, and His eternal Love will keep
that which we have committed unto Him, until that day. Is
not this a good word with which to end the year?

> Thou knewest me before I was;
>   I am all open unto Thee;
> And yet Thou lovest me, because
>   Thou, my Lord, lovest me.
>
> I may not fear, for to the end
>   Thou lovest. Who save only Thee,
> The sinner's Saviour and his Friend,
>   Would set his love on me?
>
> And on Thee now my heart is set,
>   Thy Name is music unto me.
> O help me never to forget
>   That I am loved by Thee.

TWO LITTLE SONGS FOR GOOD FRIDAY

Calvary [1]

Lord Jesus, Redeemer,
    Didst Thou die for me?
For me, Lord, a sinner,
    How could such love be?
O fairest Lord Jesus,
    Didst Thou suffer scorn?
For me, Lord, a sinner,
    Wear a crown of thorn?

And were Thy hands wounded,
    Wounded, Lord, for me?
Thy holy feet piercèd
    On the bitter Tree?
And, Lord, wast Thou thirsty,
    Thirsty, Lord, for me?
O fairest Lord Jesus,
    How could such love be?

O make my heart tender,
    Pardon, pardon me,
That ever forgetful,
    I have grievèd Thee.
I would be Thy lover,
    Taking up my cross,
Thy lover for ever,
    Come or gain or loss.

---

[1] This was written for a new convert, whose language we did not know and who knew very little English. This explains the extreme simplicity of the words.

The humbling of the Patient one—That is Rotherham's translation of a few words in Psalm 22. 24. I do not think any of us want any words to-day, but these have spoken to me with a new voice.

> Home of our hearts, lest we forget
>   What our redemption meant for Thee,
> Let our most reverent thought be set
>   Upon Thy Calvary.
>
> We, when we suffer, turn and toss
>   And seek for ease, and seek again;
> But Thou, upon Thy bitter Cross,
>   Wast firmly fixed in pain.
>
> And in our night, star-clusters shine,
>   Flowers comfort us, and joy of song;
> Nor star, nor flower, nor song was Thine,
>   But darkness three hours long.
>
> We, in our lesser mystery
>   Of lingering ill and wingèd death,
> Would fain see clear; but could we see,
>   What need would be for faith?
>
> O Lord beloved, Thy Calvary
>   Stills all our questions; come, O come,
> Where children wandering wearily
>   Have not yet found their Home.

EASTER DAY

The Lord is risen indeed, Alleluia!

Lord Christ of Easter Day, Christ the victorious,
    On this most radiant of all radiant days,
Thee do we worship, Redeemer, all-glorious,
    Offer Thee hearts' adoration and praise.

Sealed was the stone, and the rock did enfold Him,
    There in the silence of moonlight and stars,
Till the hour struck; then the tomb could not hold Him;
    Snapped like a straw death's omnipotent bars.

Evil may triumph to-day, but To-morrow
  Seeth the end of satanical strife.
Fear not and falter not; sin, pain and sorrow
  Fall when He cometh, the Christ, Prince of Life.

Sound the word over the land and the waters,
  Let it sound over the air once again;
Christ hath arisen. His sons and His daughters,
  Lift up your heads, for He cometh to reign.

FOR A TIME OF SORROW

Sorrow is one of the things that are lent, not given. A thing that is lent may be taken away; a thing that is given is not taken away. Joy is given; sorrow is lent. We are not our own, we are bought with a price, "and our sorrow is not our own" (Samuel Rutherford said this a long time ago), it is lent to us for just a little while that we may use it for eternal purposes. Then it will be taken away and everlasting joy will be our Father's gift to us, and the Lord God will wipe away all tears from off all faces. 1 Cor. 6. 19, 20 Isa. 25. 8

So let us use this "lent" thing to draw us nearer to the heart of Him Who was once a Man of Sorrows (He is not that now, but He does not forget the feeling of sorrow). Let us use it to make us more tender with others, as He was when on earth and is still, for He is touched with the feeling of our infirmities. Heb. 4. 15

EXTRA PSALM FROM THE SEPTUAGINT
(see Note for October 27th.)

"This Psalm is a genuine one of David, though supernumerary, composed when he fought in single combat with Goliad.

I was small among my brethren, and youngest in my father's house; I tended my father's sheep. My hands formed a musical instrument, and my fingers tuned a psaltery. And who shall tell my Lord? the Lord Himself, He Himself hears. He sent forth His angel, and took me from my father's sheep, and He anointed me with the oil of His anointing. My brothers were handsome and tall; but the Lord did not take pleasure in them. I went forth to meet the Philistine; and he cursed me by his idols. But I drew his own sword, and beheaded him, and removed reproach from the children of Israel."

NOTE ON PRAYER AND FASTING[1]

This note is to those to whom the idea of "prayer and fasting" is new, and who are rather puzzled about it.

First, what does it mean?

It means a determined effort to put first things first, even at the cost of some inconvenience to oneself. It means a setting of the will towards God. It means shutting out as much as possible all interrupting things. For the thing that matters is that one cares enough to have time with God, and to say *no* to that in oneself which clamours for a good meal and perhaps conversation. It is *that* which is of value to our Lord. Such a setting of the will Godward is never a vain thing. "I said not unto the seed of Jacob, Seek ye Me in vain."

Isa. 45. 19

Psa. 27. 8

But we must be in earnest. "When Thou saidst, Seek ye My face; my heart said unto Thee, Thy face, Lord, will I seek."

A few simple *Don'ts*:

1. *Don't* get into bondage about place, or position of the body. Where did our Lord spend His hours of prayer? We know how crowded and stuffy Eastern houses are; we know that sometimes, at least, He went out into the open air to a hillside; to a garden. Where did Elijah spend the long time of waiting on his God? Again, out in the open air. I have known some who could kneel for hours by a chair. I have known others who could not. David "sat before the Lord". Some find help in going out of doors and walking up and down; this was Bishop Moule's way. Some go into their room and shut their door. Do not be in bondage. Let the leaning of your mind lead you, a God-directed mind leans to what helps the spirit most.

2 Sam. 7. 18

2. *Don't* be discouraged if at first you seem to get nowhere. I think there is no command in the whole Bible so difficult to obey and so penetrating in power, as the command to be still— "Be still, and know that I am God". Many have found this so.

Psa. 46. 10

> Ah dearest Lord! I cannot pray,
> My fancy is not free;
> Unmannerly distractions come,
> And force my thoughts from Thee.

[1] Written for a special week of prayer.

The world that looks so dull all day
   Glows bright on me at prayer,
And plans that ask no thought but then
   Wake up and meet me there.

All nature one full fountain seems
   Of dreamy sight and sound,
Which, when I kneel, breaks up its deeps,
   And makes a deluge round.

My very flesh has restless fits;
   My changeful limbs conspire
With all these phantoms of the mind
   My inner self to tire.

                 Faber.

This is true. Let the tender understanding of your God enfold you. He knows the desire of your heart. Sooner or later He will fulfil it. It is written, "He will fulfil the desire of them that fear Him". "I said not unto the seed of Jacob, Seek ye Me in vain". (Thank God, for using the poor name *Jacob* there. Do you not often feel very much like the seed of Jacob? I do. "Surely, shall one say, In the Lord have I righteousness and strength". There is none of either in the seed of Jacob.)   Psa. 145. 19   Isa. 45. 19   Isa. 45. 24

3. *Don't* feel it necessary to pray all the time; listen. Solomon asked for a hearing heart. It may be that the Lord wants to search the ground of your heart, not the top layer, but the ground. Give Him time to do this. And read the Words of Life. Let them enter into you.   1 Kings 3. 9 mar.

4. *Don't* forget there is one other person interested in you—extremely interested; he will talk, probably quite vehemently, for there is no truer word than the old couplet,

       Satan trembles when he sees
       The weakest saint upon his knees.

As far as I know the only way to silence his talk is to read or say aloud (or recall to mind) counter-words, "It is written, . . . It is written, . . . It is written"; or to sing, for the devil detests song. "Singing . . . in your heart", "singing . . . to the Lord"—either or both are too much for him.   Matt. 4. 4, 7, 10   Eph. 5. 19, and   Col. 3. 16

Psa. 143. 10
P.B.V. But let the Spirit lead as to what to read. "Let Thy loving Spirit lead me forth into the land of righteousness."

5. *Don't* give up in despair if no thoughts and no words come, but only distractions and inward confusions. Often it helps to use the words of others, making them one's own. Psalm, hymn, song—use what helps most.

Psa. 127. 2
R.V. mar. 6. *Don't* worry if you fall asleep. "He giveth unto His beloved in sleep."

7. And if the day ends in what seems failure, *don't* fret. Tell Him about it. Tell Him you are sorry. Even so, don't be discouraged. All discouragement is of the devil. It is true as Faber says again :

> Had I, dear Lord, no pleasure found
>   But in the thought of Thee,
> Prayer would have come unsought, and been
>   A truer liberty.
>
> Yet Thou art oft most present, Lord,
>   In weak distracted prayer;
> A sinner out of heart with self
>   Most often finds Thee there.
>
> For prayer that humbles sets the soul
>   From all illusions free,
> And teaches it how utterly,
>   Dear Lord, it hangs on Thee.

Psa. 63. 9.
P.B.V. Then let your soul hang on Him. "My soul hangeth upon Thee"—not upon my happiness in prayer, but just upon Thee. Tell Him you are sorry, and fall back on the old words : "Lord, John 21. 17 Thou knowest all things; Thou knowest that I love Thee"— Psa. 145. 14
P.B.V. unworthy as I am. Let these words comfort your heart : "The Heb. 10. 35 Lord . . . lifteth up all those that are down." "Cast not away . . . your confidence," there is a "great recompense of reward" waiting for you a little later on.

But maybe it will be quite different. "Sometimes a light surprises the Christian when he sings," or waits with his heart

set upon access to his God; and he is bathed in wonder that
to such dust of the earth such revelations of love can be
given. If so it be, to Him be the praise. It is all of Him.

"*Now the God of peace, that brought again from the dead
our Lord Jesus, that great Shepherd of the sheep, through the
blood of the everlasting covenant, make you perfect in every
good work to do His will, working in you that which is wellpleasing in His sight, through Jesus Christ; to Whom be glory* Heb. 13. 20, 21
for ever and ever. Amen."

THE DOHNAVUR FELLOWSHIP

ORIGIN. The work in Dohnavur, South India, began in 1901, when Amy Carmichael, while doing itinerant evangelistic work, came to know that little girls were sometimes taken and trained as dancing-girls for the Hindu temples—which meant a life of evil for them. Wherever she could, she saved children from this fate, and, with her as "Mother", the Family in Dohnavur began.

In recent years good laws have been passed, and the dedication of girls to temples made illegal. Danger still exists, however, though its sources are changing and hard to trace. In spite of legislation, and both Government and private efforts, houses of ill-fame seem to be on the increase, and it is known that little girls are brought up in some of these, even from babyhood, with immoral purposes in view. Boys are also in moral danger. We make a home for any baby or older child whom we have reason to think may otherwise fall into the hands of those who would so train and use it.

OBJECTIVE. The deliverance of these children, their spiritual salvation and their training to serve others are our main objectives. Sometimes we are able to shelter older girls and women. We seek to succour the desolate and suffering, and to make the love of God and His plan of redemption in its fulness known to all whom we can reach.

WORK AND WORKERS. We are a company of people, both Indian and from overseas, men and women, married and single, whose common loyalty is to our Lord and Saviour, Jesus Christ. This binds us to one another. We have many children and young people under our care: babies, toddlers, and younger schoolboys and schoolgirls in Dohnavur; while older boys and girls, and young men and women, are receiving education and training in various institutions all over the Madras State (and even farther afield). The latter are based either on Dohnavur or on one of our out-stations. In some cases the out-station is itself a training centre. The need of shepherding them all continues till they are securely launched in life elsewhere, or have become our fellow-workers here. Some who are ill-adjusted spiritually may be a care and a problem for years, and the handicapped naturally become a permanent part of the Family.

Our Hospital provides treatment for the people of the countryside as well as for those of the Family who may be ill. From time to time we have established temporary medical outposts. The majority of the staff have grown up in our own Family.

Although we come from various denominations, we are all evangelical. We do not belong officially to any of the organized churches, but seek to serve all in our neighbourhood, and calls for help sometimes come from further afield also.

ADMINISTRATION AND FINANCE. The headquarters of the work is in Dohnavur, and we have no controlling body elsewhere. We have an Office in London, and friends in other lands act as Honorary Secretaries.

Our Heavenly Father has promised to supply all our needs according to His riches in glory by Christ Jesus. We make no appeal for funds, and do not authorize anyone to make such appeals. We have found it enough to look to Him to direct us in all things, to overcome every difficulty, and to provide for every need.

ADDRESSES
The Dohnavur Fellowship, Dohnavur, Tirunelveli District, South India
The Dohnavur Fellowship, 33 Church Road, Wimbledon, London, S.W.19

Dohnavur, 1970